WHAT OTHERS ARE SAYING ABOUT SOME OF THE SOLUTIONS IN *LEVERAGING DIGITAL TRANSFORMATION* AND ABOUT M. NADIA VINCENT

"Marie Nadia Vincent's talk on improving employee experience for better digital transformation results is spot on."

— Stella Loannidou, TaiTechSym2019

"Leading digital transformation, business, people, and IT—Excellent, Marie Vincent!"

— Paola Romero, TaiTechSym2019

"What a genuine and enjoyable presentation! Thank you for the effort you have invested in coordinating this to share. You have provided some new tools for preparing the appropriate mindset when preparing for a change in the project. It is often approached with anxiety, but you have helped give me tools to normalize it more effectively for my team and stakeholders."

— Theresa Zicker, Newmont Mining, Riverdale, Utah, USA

"Such a great presentation and subject! It's very personal, but the topic is really interesting. On top of this, the presentation is captivating. A must-see! Thanks!"

—Nicolas Bonnefous, Co-Founder of CTO/COO,
VAADATA, Lyon, France

"Thanks for the presentations. The changes status in the slide exactly depicted what I am facing. Very insightful."

— Joseph bo jiang, Country Manager,
Access Professional, Singapore

"A few good takeaways: 1. Difference between managers and leaders was very nicely presented. 2. Time, Scope, Quality and "People" - the Addition of the "People" entity was brilliant. Thank you for wonderful insight."

— Deepak Charma, Idexcel Inc, Parsippany, New Jersey, USA

"Thank you, Nadia. The webinar was very informative and will be useful in my own change management projects."

— James Eustace, Education and Training Boards, Ireland

"Good presentation! The change subject is with us in every facet of life. They say change is constant, yet resistance to change always happens. Your presentation featured good ideas on successfully driving change and is especially welcomed in today's project management world. Thanks."

— Chinagozi Efuribe, Port Harcourt, Rivers, Nigeria

"Nadia you were exceptional. Great information and delivery."

— Synthia Faulks, Covington, Georgia, USA

"Excellent presentation, Nadia. Thank you. I will definitely attend a webinar dedicated to neuroplasticity and emotional intelligence."

— Conrad D'Cruz, Netswirl Inc., Apex, North Carolina, USA

"Good presentation I can relate to easily from experience. The high point, which you stressed so well, is the need for continual IT and business alignment throughout the project".

— Henry Ogbu, Phillips Consulting Limited

"Brilliant presentation on change project management. Thanks, Nadia. I am surely gonna go through it again!"

— Prashant Sonnaik, Mediclinic Middle East

"Thanks. Agree with you that "we must have leaders with vision." Great presentation. Almost all my projects were Change Projects according to your classifications."

— Hassan Mohssine, EPMO, Bank, Toronto, Ontario, Canada

"Engaging and informative. I am enjoying how Nadia organizes these concepts and ties them together."

— Janet Dyke, Eureka Springs, Arizona, USA

"Very good. The concepts are consistent with both Lewin's 3-Step Model and Janssen's 4 Room Apartment Model of Change while delivering some good, practical advice for getting folks through the change process."

— Kevin Spurgin, Olympia, Washington, USA

"Very motivating presentation with lots of points to implement."

— Roy Cherukarayil, Consultant, Assets and Solutions,
Tata Consultancy Services, Ltd

"Excellent Presentation! One of the best I've seen to truly integrate the IT and Change Management aspects of a project."

— Daniel Lara, AmeriSpec Inspection Services,
Hernando, Mississippi, USA

"As a PM recently moved into the role of manager for Organizational Change Management, I found that this webinar gave great practical actions. It brought both together perfectly."

— Amy Byrket, Community Health Network, SPICELAN

"Outstanding.... Excellent content and facts describing what employees are experiencing in 2019. I really received much value from this presentation. From her examples, Nadia knows transformation.

The examples were substantial. The formula was great, especially, taking fear out of the process. Great presentation! Looking forward to utilizing what I've learned with my team!

— Mark Bridger

Marie Nadia has the capacity to take over a project with very little information and to drive the project until its end. She assures the deliverables are provided with quality, within the timing, and in the budgets. Above this, she is very friendly and has the possibility to get along and find pragmatic solutions with everybody."

— Philippe Hendrix, Payment Scheme Consultant, Worldline

"I have had the pleasure to work on Marie Nadia's project. Enthusiasm, vision, rapid'n'safe decisions in complex situations, and of course, positive thinking are certainly among her many qualities. She is very determined, has an eye for business, and is a diplomatic negotiator. Marie Nadia is the kind of experienced manager I would recommend to help you start up and structure your business and to boost your operational activities in a straight line."

— Faisal Iqbal, Senior Test and Quality Leader at
European Commission

LEVERAGING DIGITAL TRANSFORMATION

Proven Leadership and Innovation Strategy to Engage and Grow Your Organization

M. NADIA VINCENT, MBA

Foreword by David A. Maynard

Leveraging Digital Transformation
Proven Leadership and Innovation Strategy to Engage and Grow Your Organization

Third Edition

Published by:
Aviva Publishing
Lake Placid, NY
(518) 523-1320
www.AvivaPubs.com

Marie Nadia Vincent
Marie Nadia Vincent
Email: nvincent@digitaltransformationleaders.com
www.DigitalTransformationLeaders.com
www.LeveragingDigitalTransformation.com

ISBN: 978-1-950241-52-1 (paperback)
ISBN: 978-1-950241-66-8 (softcover)
ISBN: 978-1-950241-67-5 (ebook)
Library of Congress: 2019919981
Editor: Superior Book Productions
Cover Designer: SK Interkab Alarm
Interior Book Layout: EbookPbook
Every attempt has been made to properly source all quotes.
Printed in the United States of America
Third Edition
4 6 8 10 12 14

To my sons Alexander and Leonardo, you are my inspiration and my world.

To my nieces and nephew Anne-Rose, Jonathan, and Yva, for your love strengthens me.

To you, holding this book, may your organization or business flourish beyond your imagination and may you create prosperity and accomplishment for your team, your organization, and yourself. May you be an inspiration in the lives of many people and contribute to making our world a better place in the digital age.

ACKNOWLEDGMENTS

I would like to acknowledge the following people who each contributed somehow in making this book possible. My sons Alexander and Leonardo Home for their constant love and support—especially, for their understanding my countless work hours to make this book a reality. You two are the most amazing young men in my life. My sister Perpetue Vincent Sevère, thank you for being always reliable. You are one of my greatest gifts. My brother Pierre Robenson Vincent, thank you for your support.

Thank you to my friend Stuart Ross for your advice. Thanks to you Sergei Peleshuk, Nick Jain for your contribution. Tia Ross, Margareth Packer, thank you for your encouragement and never letting go of inspiring me. Thank you to my different editors. David A. Maynard, thank you for your strong support. Thank you, John Assaraf, for never failing to inspire me to go out of my comfort zone. You are one of the best teachers and coaches. Thank you to my PMI co-experts team for challenging my digital transformation formula first. Thank you, Penny and Andy Adams, for believing in me.

Thank you to my wonderful friends Dominique Sieradzki, Isabelle Bisson, Louise and Philippe Pourbaix, Pam and Matthew Venner, Georges Lassoie, Marie-Louise Maître, and Marie-Alice Degraff, for being a great part of my personal support. You are outstanding, and I am very grateful for you.

CONTENTS

Acknowledgments ix
Foreword xiii

Introduction: **The Digital Opportunity** **1**

Chapter One: **Embracing the New Business Intelligence for Leadership** **10**

Chapter Two: **Empowering the Digital Transformation Leader in You** **19**

Chapter Three: **Visions That Transform** **32**

Chapter Four: **Turning Your Vision Into A Mission** **46**

Chapter Five: **Announcing to Engage** **53**

Chapter Six: **Creating the Transformation Support Team** **71**

Chapter Seven: **Innovation—How I Invented the Smartphone Before Steve Jobs** **85**

Chapter Eight: **Planning Strategically End-To-End** **93**

Chapter Nine:	**Digital Transformation Strategy vs. Business Strategy**	**114**
Chapter Ten:	**Digital Transformation Strategy vs. Technology Implementation**	**130**
Chapter Eleven:	**Digital Transformation vs. Data Science**	**143**
Chapter Twelve:	**Process Streamlining for Effectiveness**	**160**
Chapter Thirteen:	**Enabling the Digital Organization**	**167**
Chapter Fourteen:	**A True Story About Cost Cutting and Effectiveness**	**178**
Chapter Fifteen:	**Digital Transformation Rescue - Cases Studies**	**183**
Chapter Sixteen:	**Embracing Artificial Intelligence: The New Frontier for Business**	**199**
Chapter Seventeen:	**Leading Job Reinvention: Building Digitally Intelligent Human-Machine Teams**	**212**

A Final Note 231
Bonus Section: The Ultimate Executive Guide for Embracing Artificial Intelligence 235
Bibliography 251
About the Author 253
About Executive Innovators Board 257
About M. Nadia Vincent Executive Advisory & Consulting Services 261
Book M. Nadia Vincent to Speak at Your Next Event 263

FOREWORD

CALLING LEADERS FROM THE BACK SEAT TO THE STEERING WHEEL

This 3rd edition of Leveraging Digital Transformation is an urgent call for leaders to take position amid AI disruption and worldwide uncertainty and transformation

ANOTHER DISRUPTION WAVE BEYOND COVID-19

We are living through a more profound disruption than anything in recent history, even greater than the upheaval of COVID-19 that took us by surprise.

The second **edition of *Leveraging Digital Transformation*** was published just as the world was about to change at the beginning of year 2020. In January 2020, I was preparing for an international book tour. The first stop was Dubai.

While there, I began hearing news about an epidemic in China.

At the airport, I saw something unusual, massive groups of Asian travelers travelling together, all wearing protective masks. Not scattered individuals, but entire groups.

"That moment, I realized that the big digital tsunami I had predicted was already happening."

THE PREDICTION BEFORE THE TSUNAMI

Just two months earlier, Thinkers360 had asked me to share my predictions for 2020. My warning was clear:

"In 2020, businesses that have transformed their enterprise entirely will distance themselves from those that have implemented only partial digital transformation. The Second Machine Age Tsunami will submerge the laggards. Disrupted enterprises will be unable to compete with organizations that are transformed, inspired, well-led, and fully leveraging every chord of innovation. Executives must take urgent strategic action now to transform their entire organization, move at the speed of innovation, and secure their place among successful digital enterprises."— *Nadia Vincent, MBA, Digital Transformation Executive Advisor, MIT Sloan Certified Executive Strategy & Innovation, CEO Digitrans Management & Leadership Ltd*

THE SECOND MACHINE AGE TSUNAMI HAD ARRIVED AND HAD A NAME: COVID-19

When COVID-19 hit, it became that Second Machine Age Tsunami. For businesses not yet transformed, it was a brutal ultimatum: **change now or never**.

Technology was ready, like a modern-day Noah's Ark, but leaders had to decide whether to board or drown.

The pandemic revealed more than the state of our technology; it revealed the **state of our leadership**, agility, innovation capacity, flexibility, endurance, empathy, and the digital maturity of organizations.

Leadership was the real differentiator.

Some companies transitioned quickly to remote work, serving customers seamlessly while behind the scenes, teams navigated massive change. Others closed permanently, sold under pressure, or never regained their pre-COVID footing.

FROM PANDEMIC TO AI DISRUPTION

Even organizations that adapted well to the pandemic now face new waves of disruption of various sorts. They are facing one or more disruptions related to geopolitical instability, wars, economic volatility, global inflation, environmental crises, trade wars, and rapid technological shifts, massive layoffs and artificial intelligence business automation.

But the most significant disruption today, the **Third Machine Age Tsunami** is the **rise of artificial intelligence**.

The AI of 2020 and the AI of 2025 are vastly different. What we will see between 2026 and 2030 will be another leap entirely. Artificial Intelligence is advancing at a speed that rivals, and in some cases surpasses, human capability. The level of fear I describe in the digital transformation formula in the first chapter of this book is at its top. The need of authentic digital leadership is beyond urgent. It is critical.

MIT Sloan has published a report earlier this year (2025) that reveals that 95% of AI implementations in enterprise fail or have no measurable effects on P&L (Profit and Loss). This report confirms how critical the need to reignite digital leadership in our businesses and organizations.

THE DIGITAL TRANSFORMATION SUCCESS FORMULA

I created the digital transformation success formula ten years ago back in 2015 in the early years when we moved away from changes and labeled them digital transformation. This book is written around that formula. You will learn more about it in detail further.

Digital Transformation = Individual Transformation × Business Transformation × Technology Transformation ÷ Fear

Today, fear is at its peak. Many leaders and organizations have shifted into **defensive mode**, investing less, automating to cut costs, and treating technology as a shield instead of a growth driver. This approach often results in flawed automation and stalled innovation.

Two Types of Organizations

- **Defensive Organizations**
    - Automate to survive, not to grow.
    - Keep the status quo.
    - Reduce investment in people.
    - Let fear dictate strategy.

- **Futuristic Organizations**
    - Use automation strategically to grow
    - Invest in people's agility and adaptability.
    - Reinvent roles for the future.
    - Make changes with purpose, not panic.

THE LEADERSHIP GAP

Right now, AI's voice is louder than leadership's. Many leaders have stepped back into "watch and see" mode, allowing fear and uncertainty to slow innovation.

But technology will keep advancing, with or without leadership engagement. Leaders must step forward, not to ignore risks, but to assess them, manage them, innovate, inspire people, and create the **next digital reality**.

THE HUMAN QUESTION

If AI can do so much, and often better than humans, what is the role of humans today?How do leaders inspire trust in times of disruption?

The answer: **human roles have changed**. We are being called to **elevate our consciousness**.

Our brains are wired for self-protection, defaulting to fight-or-flight when faced with uncertainty. But in this era, neither fight nor flight is enough. The answer is **elevation.** We are called to rise above fear, embrace higher-purpose leadership, and direct our unique human capabilities toward solving meaningful problems.

WHY DIGITAL TRANSFORMATION STILL MATTERS MORE THAN EVER

Some believe AI has made digital transformation obsolete, that AI is the "new trend." This is dangerously wrong.

AI is part of digital transformation, not a replacement for it. In fact, it demands **more digital leadership** because it forces us to reinvent strategies, organizations, and our sense of purpose.

That's why this third edition is now **Leveraging Digital Transformation and AI**. AI is the most disruptive technology of our time, but when combined with visionary leadership, it is also the most powerful tool for creating the future.

OUR LEADERSHIP MISSION

We must:

Revive digital transformation leadership to

- Lead with courage in chaotic times
- Harness AI to create value, not fear
- Inspire trust by focusing on human purpose & problem solving
- Innovate and create the future

Leveraging Digital Transformation was written ahead of this time today, for today and the future.

We have the tools. We have the opportunity. We have the responsibility to create the future.Leaders, we have work to do. Let's go!

Marie Nadia Vincent

Our deepest fear is not that we are inadequate. Our deepest fear is that we are powerful beyond measure.

It is our light, not our darkness, that most frightens us.

We ask ourselves, who am I to be brilliant, gorgeous, talented, and fabulous? Actually, who are you not to be? You are a child of God. You playing small does not serve the world. There is nothing enlightened about shrinking so that other people will not feel insecure around you.

We are all meant to shine, as children do. We were born to make manifest the glory of God that is within us. It is not just in some of us; it is in everyone, and as we let our own light shine, we unconsciously give others permission to do the same. As we are liberated from our own fear, our presence automatically liberates others.

— Marianne Williamson

INTRODUCTION

The Digital Opportunity

"Growth is the only Evidence of Life".

- JOHN HENRI NEWMAN

It was twenty years ago. I was a young business and technology analyst at the global banking corporation, Swift, working on a main CRM project. That last trimester of 1999 was nothing like the previous one. Wherever you turned in businesses or the media, there were two dominant conversations: one gave hope for a united Europe, even with some international concerns, and the other sent scary vibes in everyone's body. The first was the adoption of the unique Euro money for the eurozone and the other, the Y2K bug.

The stories and warnings I heard about the Y2K bug were frightening. It was reported that everything computer-operated would either break down or experience major turbulence. People were warned not to be in an elevator around midnight, to avoid flying that night, to print and keep secured all statements of bank accounts and assets, and the list goes on. Facebook and Twitter did not exist, but online forums were filled with these discussions.

At work, there was the same phobia, but we did not know precisely what to fear or how it would break our system. I did not work at night, only during business hours. However, all the IT department was on alert mode. When my manager asked for a night duty person for New Year's Eve, I was delighted to have an opportunity to confront that Y2K face to face, so I quickly said, "Yes, I'll come." I have always had the gene of an innovator, and new challenges give me a wonderful thrill. Although the Y2K bug was explained, I still could not grasp the logical explanation of why it would happen, what would cause it, and how to prevent it. So I did like everyone else, meaning doing my job correctly and hoping for the best, despite the buzz.

New Year's Eve, I got to the office early that evening. My work was polished. I verified all systems I was working with, and they were working, as usual—nothing to signal. I liaisoned with several colleagues in different teams and departments—nothing alarming. We were there, waiting, not knowing exactly what to expect. Would all the lights go off? Would the badge-automated access doors system in the building fail? Would the whole IT system fail? Would the elevators fail? Nobody knew. We waited to see.

Some managers arranged for a New Year's celebration wherever it can take place. At our desks, in the offices, in the hallways, wherever that can be. Therefore, many bottles of champagne and some snacks were in stock for the employees on each floor. That gave a light spirit to the worrying context.

Midnight came, and the building lights remained on; the systems functioned correctly, the automated doors worked as usual, and nobody wanted to try the elevators until much later, and when they did, they worked fine. Our multiple IT systems worked correctly, and it was business as usual. In the news, on the internet, even for the Asian countries that entered the new millennium before us in Europe, nothing happened. Our colleagues in the USA in Virginia started to take it easy as we told them everything was as usual, and they could not see any issue on their side either. The troubled spirit has given place to a celebratory one. Cheers being made with champagne glasses, waves of laughter, and wishes of "Happy New Year" filled the air. Nothing we worried about had happened.

I was happy to go smoothly into the New Year, but the part of me that wanted to learn something new and deploy my innovative and problem-solving skills was disappointed. I thought, *Well, I'll have another opportunity with the change to the Euro. At least, this is very real and specific. Welcome year 2000! Welcome new millennium! Bring real business challenges for my problem-solving and innovation skills.*

Business challenges and opportunities there were plenty. As a consultant, I had the chance to work with different clients, thus enjoying more challenging but richer experiences. There was the Euro, but also all the various legislative changes that came with it. Then globalization brought considerable changes to the world, forcing many business mergers and acquisitions, eliminating most monopolies, and making space on the market for new entrants in many sectors. Paper statements had been replaced in countless businesses and administrations, in exchange for digital experiences. Hackers had grown their businesses as well, and hacking became common for organizations. A new shift happened in technology, forcing more regulations on more advanced security procedures such as advanced data encryption,

PCI technologies, and more. The business landscape had changed dramatically.

But this was only the introduction to the digital age and preparation for the real transformation that is now taking place, twenty years later.

Welcome to the second machine age, the age when the machine gets smart and smarter. The smartphone revolutionizes everything, and cloud technology, mobility, social media, virtual technologies, and data science have brought tremendous value. Artificial intelligence is awakened from its wintering to take advantage of all the outbursts of technologies available. Every day, more technology and business innovations are disrupting our world.

Technology is creating new opportunities to change our world; however, the transformation coming is an accumulative function of four main pillars: leadership, business strategy, innovation strategy and technology. I am inviting you to leverage digital transformation by taking into account those four pillars.

In the first edition of this book, I brought you the digital transformation success formula. It is still the best formula to achieve sustainable business transformation. Now, I'll take it further to get you to leverage digital transformation, using the success formula. In the end, I will show you in some case studies the top five mistakes that businesses that invested in digital transformation make, the parts that they miss from the formula, and how I rescued them.

Thank you for reading this book. Now, what are you creating for your organization, your team, or your loved ones? Let me help you make it a rewarding reality.

DT = IT X BT X TT/F

Digital Transformation = Individual Transformation x (multiplied by) Business Transformation x (multiplied by) Technology Transformation / (divided by) Fears

Digital Transformation is equal to Individual Transformation, multiplied by Business Transformation, multiplied by Technology Transformation and divided by Fears.

The components that make or break digital transformation, as outlined in the equation, are:

1. Individual transformation
2. Business vision and strategy for transformation and innovation
3. Technology implementation and usage
4. Fear reduction and management throughout the process.

The first factor, individual transformation, must be met first by the leader before expecting transformation from the rest of the organization or collaborators.

The strategic business transformation vision must be created by the "transformed" leader so that it is transformative for the business or organization.

The technology transformation strategy must reflect the business' strategic vision.

Fear, the emotion that leads to countless other negative emotions, restricts individuals and compromises transformation. It must be reduced, managed, and recycled into positive energy throughout the whole transformation process.

I address all these factors in a practical way to help you, the leader, as you strategize and implement digital transformation in your organization.

Two decades in management and technology consultancy in medium to large organizations has taught me how the biggest challenges encountered during any part of a business or project lifecycle are more human related than technology related. Our number one mistake is to rely too much on the technology.

No amount of technology can substitute for poor business strategies and failures in work collaboration. The lack of communication and collaboration costs large companies millions, despite the fact that everyone has phones on their desks and a plethora of communication, business, and technology tools on their computers.

I have worked mostly as an external consultant, implementing medium and large technology and business projects in Fortune 500 companies internationally. I am mostly called in to lead or rescue large projects that the client organizations have trouble delivering. Often, several managers preceded me who did not or could not deliver as expected. I have been the rescue leader about 80 percent of the time in my career. These are generally intense situations where, after I am done delivering, going on a vacation is the most appropriate thing to do. What I've realized over the years is that there has been a pattern in these professional assignments—they were change or transformation projects that were not similar to any other projects in the organization, so the people in the organization were not prepared for them or refused to embrace them.

No matter the reason, I found that by addressing the individual, the business, and the technology elements in my leadership strategy, I always succeeded. That is, until a failure occurred, and I realized something was missing in the equation. It took me yet another failure to search further, learn much more, and get the equation right.

What I did not know is I was being trained in the subject of change and transformation throughout my career without even knowing it.

I am someone who likes to get to the point and get things done! Getting results is very important to me in whatever I am doing. In fact, it is about more than getting results—it is about getting *meaningful* results. I like to contribute to something positive and constructive, and if I realize I am not doing that with whatever project I've undertaken, then it is time again for change. Being a consultant has been the perfect career choice for me because it has allowed me to contribute to different organizations at different moments in their lifetimes, and I have learned much more than if I were just an employee in the same organization for two decades. To the surprise of many, I have never looked for the job security of obtaining a permanent employee position in one of the large organizations I had the opportunity to work for. My motivation came from how I was helping the organization reach its goals and where my services were most needed.

One skill that has been key for me in delivering large and challenging projects in the timeframe of one year or a maximum of two years (occasionally less than a year) is the ability to quickly grasp and understand the organization's knowledge in terms of business, people, technology, and culture. I realize transition periods are not the same for everyone; many individuals may need six months to a year in an organization before they can productively perform. I almost never have that opportunity. I am generally hired to deliver yesterday. Is that an accident? No, I don't think so. That's the type of consultancy mission I've attracted because of my beliefs and high expectations for myself. This workstyle is sometimes draining and kicks me out of balance. But I prefer harmony over balance.

I am not smarter than you. I say that because I am not here to brag. I am here to help you understand that transformation will require the same abilities I have and use from you.

Maybe I acquired my abilities because I was so curious about the world, dreamed of experiencing and got to experience life on two continents in four countries, and have experienced my share of failures and successes in life. Through the process, I learned to speak four languages (and I can communicate a little in two other languages). I have managed international and global projects, collaborating with people of more nationalities and backgrounds than I can count. But whatever reason prepared me for these experiences, the most important element is that I have always been open. I have always been open to learn, open about people and possibilities, and open to contributing to others as much, if not more, than I gracefully receive.

I stayed open to be more, despite challenges and failures that could have made me quit; instead, I used them as leverage.

As a digital transformation leader, you must be open—open to transform yourself first so you can help transform others and thus help transform our world for the best. We digital transformation leaders are to lead the way to transformation for our people, not command them where to go. Remember that!

The digital opportunity is for each of us. Regardless of how it looks like upfront, opportunities exist for everyone—even for those who do not see those opportunities yet. As we lead our people to find opportunities and thrive in transformation, we will also inspire, and when required, release them to find their opportunities elsewhere.

My goal with this book is to inspire, guide, and lead you as you lead other leaders and professionals to create digital transformation. I won't be entertaining you with great and long literature. This book is meant to be a short and practical read with a long action list that will inspire you to create a digitally transformed organization. Thank you for giving me the opportunity to contribute to your knowledge, skills, and success.

Let's get started!

Marie Nadia VINCENT

CHAPTER ONE

Embracing the New Business Intelligence for Leadership

"We should not only use the brains we have, but all that we can borrow."

— WOODROW WILSON

Digital transformation has been going on for more than twenty years now, so what's new about it?

Over the last thirty-plus years, we had the first machine age, and that focused on transforming the power system or the workforce. Think about the end of the industrial revolution and the start of the digital revolution. We switched from manual tasks to computer operated tasks.

Today, we are in the second machine age. The second machine age is about transforming the control system of the business or the governance transformation.

In that second machine age, we see genuine business transformations like never before. The newest digital technologies facilitate changes in business models, business operation, and business intelligence. Many aspects of science fiction are turning into realities.

Many businesses that would have failed in the first machine age are succeeding globally in the second machine age. The largest supermarket in the world, Amazon, has no private inventory; the largest hotel chain, Airbnb, has no building of its own; the largest taxi company, Uber, has no vehicles of its own. We also have the gig economy that has reinvented jobs and employment globally with online platforms such as Fiverr.com, for example. The platform allows anyone, and especially freelancers, to sell their services online directly to clients anywhere in the world and at the most competitive prices.

Countless enterprises have gone out of business because of the gig economy. On the other hand, the digital businesses mentioned above have succeeded due to their easy accessibility, competitive pricing, and better customer experience. The business landscape is continuously transforming and innovating fast, for every sector and, only the fittest, the smartest, and the most innovative enterprises will survive in the next five to ten years.

It gets even more exciting than that with the technologies of extreme decentralization such as bitcoins and blockchain. The largest peer to peer electronic cash system, bitcoin, is entirely decentralized and with a ledger that is also wholly secured and decentralized, the blockchain. While the bitcoin electronic cash system was the main focus, the blockchain technology creates another new revolution of its own for it is even more attractive for global businesses than bitcoin.

We are in a new economy, the shared economy, powered by amazing digital technologies. This is only the start of the digital transformation that is taking place in our world.

What digital transformation means for you as an executive is that the control system has changed; the economic system has changed. The economic principles that we learned in business school, while still relevant for many, are being overshadowed. There are many more new ways to do business that are in line with today's realities, and they are made possible by technology.

I am both a business and a technology major, and I have worked mostly on the technology side, implementing breakthrough digital solutions for businesses. I can tell you that, without the right business strategy, the technology becomes irrelevant. Often, I had to help the business gain clarity about what they are trying to achieve with the technology to guarantee a successful outcome. However, many Fortune companies waste millions on process and technology implementations that end up being totally out of line with their business vision, or worse, that they do not have a focused vision at all. Many organizations, especially large ones, are confused by technology, and that can be very costly for them. I don't want that for you, and this book is meant to guide you in leveraging technology. I want you to remember that:

1. The digital transformation is powered by technology, but it is created by innovative strategy.
2. Today business intelligence is not just human anymore but requires the right combination of human and artificial intelligence.

3. Human intelligence and artificial intelligence are not equal and not interchangeable. They are complementary. Each can focus on what they do best.
4. Innovative vital strategies will help you take advantage of the new business intelligence and redefine your control system and maybe even your power (operation) system.

I have great news for you about the possibilities you can tap into now—all available at once, unlike before.

1. You don't have to make the most significant business decisions on your own anymore. Yes, you still have this full power. Smile! You won't have to go with guesswork anymore. Data-driven decision making will give you a potent edge.
2. You don't have to delay making decisions due to unknown risk levels. Your risk management can be controlled automatically.
3. You have more power (horsepower, brainpower, computer power, artificial brainpower, robot power) available now to get the job done effectively and fast. How you arrange this power becomes your innovative business model.
4. Your power base can be decentralized without affecting work quality if, and only if, you align your model correctly and build the appropriate business ecosystem.
5. You don't have to worry about uncertainty down the line; you can monitor progress from where you are and even take corrective actions.
6. You know Murphy of the infamous law and how he's always lurking, waiting, leaving you begging him to go away? With proper strategies planned and in place beforehand, you can eliminate many of the "can go wrongs," leaving Murphy with few "will go wrongs."

7. Above, I talked about arranging your power to create your business model. Beyond that, you can start identifying potential revenue streams by reviewing your value proposition. The notion of value has changed in every sector.
8. Before, your investments were uncertain; you didn't know which would generate profits and which would drain your finances, or you didn't know when to make which investments. Now, you can identify your cash cows, your financial drains, your bottlenecks, and you can even predict them and anticipate which will be dead-end investments and which will be innovative successes. Isn't that a great news?
9. Your organization can be innovative, fast to deliver, excited, and engaged with each new venture, driving implementations at a rapid pace if, and only if, you invest in individuals, so they are engaged and benefit from the opportunities of the digital age, instead of being restrained by the fear of losing advantages acquired, promised, or foreseen in the past industrial age.
10. Your customers can become your primary source of innovative ideas, your advocate, and support your product development, even contribute to it. They may market your products and business for you—if, and only if, you provide exciting and rewarding customer experiences.
11. With all the possibilities, tools, and new, empowering innovation technologies coming out every day, as an executive, you are in position to write your name in history as a great innovator, a great leader who people will remember as a model for many generations to come.

You must also use your brainpower and empathetic, heart-centered power to lead your organization, inspiring, and may I say, reassuring your team. Being reassuring is big in a context where many jobs are being automated and people are being made redundant. I've provided some solutions in Chapter 4, where I invite you to turn people into missionaries for digital transformation. I also point out that, for some, the change does not fit. When someone is not onboard, it is not about firing them; it's about how to release them so they can find their new purpose. The digital era is not about making humans feel insignificant—it is a call to use more of our unequaled brainpower to aim higher and achieve significant things while delegating menial tasks to machines. Just as you, the executive, take a higher view, focusing your intellect on further innovation, so to do the people in your organization. They are called to use their brainpower in higher roles, either within your organization or elsewhere. That is the digital or machine age. We are being called to a higher purpose in the universe. This is an age of abundance and possibilities!

That is a lot to change, learn, plan, and implement, you may think. Well, I'll tell you, yes, it is, but it is exciting and rewarding if you look at the fantastic opportunities you can reap from transformation. The good news is you don't have to imagine it, research it, or do it all by yourself. There are people like myself who have taken the time to learn, research, experiment, and innovate at different levels, and we are here to advise you, help you, and support you. Pick someone with technology implementation experience to advise you because there is a big gap between strategy and implementation, and the best strategists are those who have implementation experience as well. Trust me. I've seen the results and counseled executives who found themselves in critical situations. I prefer to help you beforehand, instead of coming to your rescue after you've been left hanging through inexperience.

At one point, almost every call I got was a rescue situation. As a management consultant, a continuous learner, and strategic thinker, I focus on stepping above and beyond the here and now and helping clients conceive and implement solid foundations on which their business systems can thrive. Strangely, as I write this, I am working on a plan to salvage a digital transformation situation again, and I have, without exception, encountered each challenge I warned about in *The Digital Transformation Success Formula*. It is a clear sign that many organizations around the world are struggling with transformation. And this struggle is expensive.

It is excellent that you have this book in hand. I applaud you. Now I invite you to take a step farther with implementation. Do not neglect any part of the business transformation formula. It is the secret of transformation success through the business strategy, the technology transformation, the individual transformation, and reducing the fear factor in individuals to allow them to unleash the power of digital transformation. Take action! Even if it starts with a speaking event with me or another professional to align your organization with the digital age, do it. Transformation is a process, and only when you engage in it and shift to the next phase can you truly benefit from it. This is why I add an "Action" section at the end of each chapter of this book and the previous edition *The Digital Transformation Success Formula*. Unfortunately, many organizations take a partial approach and neglect the individual transformation. And that is wrong. You must take action to be rewarded but don't overlook any aspect of the digital transformation formula because if you do, your organization will pay the price.

With new technology and the fear factor, many things that used to be "common sense" are not common sense anymore. Also, fear has many faces—some we do not recognize as fear. I've elaborated on that on Chapter 5. Therefore, when going through change and transformation, it is essential we support the individual in their transformation along with the organization's.

ETHICS

In this call to take a higher role, there is a crucial concern, though, and it is about ethics. Are there limits on what we should and should not do? While there may be no limit to what we can do, as humans, it comes back our humanity, our heart-centered presence, our conscience. We were given a conscience to help us place limits on ourselves and what we do, where we go. Moreover, when we don't follow that internal guide, we create our downfall or the downfall of our humanity. So, ethics are essential to protecting us as humans but also to living gratefully, appreciating what we receive in the universe, on the earth, and through the people we love—all the great things we enjoy.

When we bypass ethics to satisfy our ego and reject the respect—the care—that we should have for each other, we create adverse phenomena with dramatic consequences for us as humans but also for the flora, the fauna, and the overall ecosystem in which we live.

Looking at history, when we have bypassed ethics, we humans have created phenomena such as abject poverty, wars, famine, racism, crime, deforestation, discrimination, pollution, migration, poisoned land, child labor, injustice, dramatic climate change, elimination of animal and plant species, animal abuse, wildfires, human slavery, many illnesses, and wasted natural resources, and we have faced their painful consequences. So, there is no limit in the vast and wonderful things you can create, but there might be equal or worse adverse consequences in creating evil things that satisfy our ego but are counter to the well-being of others with whom we share planet earth.

In conclusion, as an executive, you have a powerful new intelligence at your disposal that could let you focus your intellect on more significant, innovative endeavors to benefit your organization. You can do amazing things, and there are no limits to what you can do, but there are consequences to what you choose to do. If we do not suffer the consequences today, we leave them to our children, grandchildren, great-grandchildren, or people on the other side of the world for many generations to come. Be brilliant, be innovative, be inspiring, and remember to satisfy not only your short-lived ego but, especially, the good of humanity. Then, it is humanity that will remember the best side of you when your ego has left this life.

CHAPTER TWO

Empowering the Digital Transformation Leader in You

No matter how busy you are, how many deadlines you are facing, or how many people are vying for your time, give yourself permission to reflect on what being a great leader means to you.

— *Douglas Ready*

Despite all the buzz about the great digital technologies we have today and how they are transforming our organizations, our businesses, and our lives, when it comes to business, there is just one competitive advantage that sets great companies apart—great leadership!

Technology allows us to automate many processes and jobs, reach and sell directly to our prospects, and build communities to engage our customers. However, technology itself has become so accessible that it is not a real competitive advantage anymore. The most effective technologies are available free or for a small investment, compared to how it was a decade ago. What makes an organization competitive now is more about having a leader who can choose the right tools to empower the business' vision and create and implement strategies to propel the organization to reaching its business objectives. In the past, many outrageously priced and misaligned (but functional) technology investments have failed to support the business' vision of their organization—some to the point of bringing down the companies.

Gone is the time when businesses and organizations had to invest in large, expensive technologies to run their operations smoothly. The digital age renders technology shareable and available on a consumer level, so organizations can now pay for systems on a per-use basis, instead of acquiring and maintaining much more expensive systems. Today, even small businesses can access the same types of technology and business-processing tools as the large organizations who create their own technologies and business-intelligence systems.

Companies like Amazon, Google, and countless others have broken the barriers for cloud computing, storage, data analytics, and business processing, so much so that the small business leader with a grand vision and plenty of audacity can compete with giant companies and even disrupt their industries.

Technology, mixed with great strategies, has already replaced reduced headcounts in organizations. Many processes, regardless of the industry, once they are well understood and executed, can be automated. As a result, many functions are now reduced to tasks related to monitoring, maintenance, and troubleshooting. While many job positions have disappeared in organizations because of this, there are also many new positions being created daily. A leader's ability to get the right skills onboard and to successfully automate what can be automated becomes crucial for an organization's productivity and success. This is proper leadership and resource management.

Managing human resources means making the best of the people involved. Changes in job functions should not always mean turnover and firing employees. Great leaders inspire their employees to be more and serve the business' needs in different job positions over time. It takes genuine leadership to help transform people to be more than just job-position holders, but to instead become the smart, flexible, skillful, and unmatched resource that we humans can be with our brain power. People will *not* go as far as they can or achieve as much as they can. They will only go as far as their leaders can take them.

It takes a transformed person to navigate a digital organization successfully. True transformation happens first for the individual, then the teams, followed by the organization. Transforming an organization is a process that is as valuable, if not more so, as implementing digital technologies and new business processes. That is because transformed people keep the vision alive and continue to innovate in an era where innovation is the new currency.

Great leaders are capable of successfully changing the user experience and turning a company's fate around; mobilizing an organization to create profound, lasting, and profitable transformations; and disrupting a whole industry with just one business innovation.

Organizations have a few prime assets, and regardless of their other assets, they must have great leaders.

THE LEADERS WE FOLLOW

We follow leaders because of their expertise, vision, beliefs, trustworthiness, self-assurance, and confidence in the vision and their perceived capacity to direct people in achieving the vision.

The above are criteria that people take into account when deciding to follow or not follow a leader, especially when they have the freedom to choose. This is valid for any organization or group. People want to follow a leader who advocates a vision that will "give" them more. It may be more power, a better work position, higher salary, greater benefits, more time to be with family, or just the opportunity to be more. Because we naturally prefer immediate gratification, we prefer to have every benefit we can receive from our organizations and our leaders right away. Therefore, seeking to "become more" is left in the last position.

Unfortunately, transformation does not give immediate gratification. Transformation is a change process during which we are transformed as much as the business or organization we are part of. During a transformation, we face many challenges, and the organization relies on the leaders to facilitate the process and achieve the vision. It is the challenges and how we approach them, how we optimize our resources, and the lessons learned, that lead to the transformation. The role requires that you strengthen yourself and become more first.

Leading digital transformation is a process during which you, as a leader, must:

1. lead your people to "become more" and be transformed; and
2. optimize your resources to achieve the business' or organization's transformative vision.

LEADING YOUR PEOPLE TO TRANSFORMATION

The most challenging aspect will be leading your people. Becoming more is gaining the inner capacity necessary for leading in stressful and challenging situations during the transformation process. Your capacity to provide reliable directions and support during the unsettling phases of the transformation process is crucial. You must be able to understand and communicate with your stakeholders—which includes people such as investors, other leaders, colleagues, peers, clients, and so on—in order to reassure them during their periods of doubt and transition. You must also know when and how to inspire, guide, and push your followers and leaders to develop resilience, to experience more, and become more as well.

A quiet sea never makes a skillful sailor.

Like the process that creates a skillful sailor, no change implementation or transformation is done without challenges. In fact, Murphy's Law is really present in transformation. Whatever can go wrong, will go wrong at the worst times. Therefore, the only way is for the leader to be prepared to handle whatever challenges occur.

Overcoming challenge is part of the process. Challenges will come from different areas and concerns: financial setbacks, stakeholders, conflicts of interest, technological failures, communication breakdowns, people challenges, lack of information, organizational structure, coordination, tools knowledge, disagreements, and so forth.

You name it. The only way out of chaos during transformation is through genuine leadership.

Becoming more is the path that leads to transformation, but it is not a straight path. As a leader, you must agree to face things that feel uncomfortable and some that even hurt. You must agree to face yourself with humility, self-acceptance, and care.

Most importantly, you must take action to transform yourself first.

The genuine leader is set on a constant journey of learning, self-improvement, and self-discovery; that is an integrated part of the job. While self-confidence is a must, humility is also a key requirement in order to keep learning and achieving greater things.

The digital transformation leader must achieve a harmonious blend of skills in leadership, business management, information technology, emotional intelligence, professional or industry knowledge, people knowledge, general knowledge, and awareness. Despite the above requirements, it is not a balance of skills, and the digital transformation leaders are not expected to be leading the transformation all by themselves. Great leaders build a leadership team around themselves consisting of other leaders with specialized knowledge to support them in the endeavor. We will show you how to create your leadership team later in the book.

If you want transformation for yourself and for your organization, you must become more and help your people to become more as well, so that you can be in a transformed reality.

Transforming people and organizations starts by first transforming yourself. Don't expect change from others if you are not changing yourself. The digital transformation leader must inspire people to grow and create the transformation. They must lead by example, meaning that their actions should be the same as their instructions for followers.

The time has passed when leaders had the most power and authority over people in an organization. Times have changed, and now, the leader is being replaced faster than ever before. But do you know why? It is because people go as fast as their leader and do as well as their leader can inspire them to do!

They will not do as great as they can or reach their potential without the inspiration they draw from their leader. The leader sets the pace, sets the level of performance, and sets the standards. Therefore, when the organization is not doing well or is not going in the expected direction, it is an indication that the leader is not inspiring enough or not leading in the right direction. In time, such leaders are replaced.

THE NUMBER ONE CONSTRAINT TO THE GROWTH OF ANY ORGANIZATION

The number one constraint to the growth of any organization is leadership. The same goes for transformation. In addition, the number one key to successful transformation is also the leader.

Have you seen how often some CIOs (Chief Information Officer) are replaced in large IT organizations around the world?

That's right—very often! It is challenging to be a CIO in a changing environment, especially if the organization is not ready for change. It is so even for the best CIOs! It takes boldness, courage, and self-preparation to make an organization shift direction successfully—that is, after the prerequisite phase of knowing which direction to go, when a vision is clearly defined, and they have the buy-in of the stakeholders. Many CIOs do not even make it past this prerequisite phase before they are replaced.

CIOs are called to be leaders, entrepreneurs, great visionaries, and technologists as well as business executives all at once. They must be all that for both organizations that are ready to change and organizations that are not, or even worse—for organizations that boycott the CIO's work. CIOs experience change in their organization the most because of the speed of change in the technology industry.

The CIO role was one of the most challenging roles until the role of the digital transformation leader was introduced. The position of digital transformation leader is not a business role or a technology role. The digital transformation leader is a hybrid role. The digital transformation leader, no matter what that position is called in your organization, is accountable for bringing that business and organization into the digital era. They are responsible for transforming people, business, and technology and ensuring that the business survives in the digital age. That is simply because businesses and organizations have two options only—transform or die.

As a leader, remind yourself that the number one constraint to your team, department, or unit is you. It is not about the situation you are facing or the business that you are in, but about what you do about it. Commit to helping your team achieve their greatest potential by aiming for *your* greatest potential.

As a transformational leader, you are called to lead by example and show the way. It is your responsibility to set the standards, the pace, and the performance level right from the start. Not everyone in the organization will like where you set the bar and some will work against you before you even start. Some will hate you for no reason other than you are taking them out of their comfort zone. Guess what? That's part of the transformation, and you are not in a popularity contest. You are not there to be liked by everyone but to inspire and transform others and your organization.

Change causes discomfort, fear, resistance, and emotional turmoil, so it is not a popular thing. You will have to be emotionally intelligent to keep from getting lost along with people who are fighting their own emotional wars. Instead, you will help them win their emotional war without getting personally involved in it. This is the fear part of the formula. You must reduce this fear throughout the whole transformation process. I'll show you how as we progress.

After all, their resistance, their fight, or their "giving up" is not about you. Most of the organization will resist leaving their comfort zone at first, and that is normal because they are human.

TAKE ADVANTAGE OF THE LATEST BRAIN-SCIENCE DISCOVERIES

Brain science demonstrates that our brain's primary function is survival. Our brain will warn us about or even reject new things that take us out of our zone of comfort, to protect us from the new thing which might be a threat to our survival. We are in a very advanced time, but we still have the same brain that protected us in when we were living in the wild, chasing things to eat, and defending ourselves against wild animals and natural threats.

If you have been around long enough to remember the old 386 computers, imagine surfing the internet, Skyping, and watching a YouTube video with a 386, Windows 3.1, Netscape, an old modem, and a phone line. We would most likely give up. That was barely twenty years ago, and the 386 is now so outdated that the thought of it amuses me. However, we've now adapted to our new systems, and the old systems are just a distant memory.

We have a primitive brain that we are using in the digital era. It requires us to make some serious adjustments. Besides adapting to new technology, people are also reconfiguring their inner systems, installing new software, and migrating to new technologies in their brain. Expect some mess, failures, testing, and trial before the transformed self takes over.

As a good leader, spend more time leading and inspiring than fighting people's resistance and emotional reactions. Lead mostly by setting the example to follow.

Monkey see; monkey do.

ENDING THE RESISTANCE FROM LEADERSHIP

Is there another leader who is somehow undermining the organization's digital transformation initiative? If so, show empathy while working to move past the blockage. If the obstacle is insurmountable, work with the rest of leadership to remove the obstacle and move on. To do so, you may need additional authority or have access to it.

You must always have the support of top management, the C-suite, in your role as a digital transformation leader. If you haven't yet, go ahead and create your steering committee with top management executives.

Prepare for and remove major threats and obstacles to transformation, and you are likely to succeed—fair or not, it's still up to you to deal with peers and higher ups who are not onboard and may cause a blockage. Remember, you don't need popularity; change is not popular while it's happening. You need transformation, and you are fully responsible for making it happen.

Keep leading, inspiring, performing, and helping others grow. Set the standards, set the pace, lead by example, show empathy, walk your talk, and transform!

OPTIMIZING YOUR RESOURCES

The information-technology field is one of the most innovative sectors, yet it has one of the highest failure rates when it comes to project management. The technology itself may be seen as the cause of these failures, yet, in fact, as with many other fields, the issue is usually people.

Optimizing resources is highly dependent on managing and leading people. Technology can hardly fail us, since technology executes what we tell it to execute. The same goes for other resources that we manage, such as financial, business, professional, natural, and technology resources. We can manage and optimize them by learning more about their properties and behaviors.

Finding, optimizing, and controlling our resources is also a priority for the digital transformation leader. Controlling and optimizing our disparate resources requires us to have more information about their properties, behaviors, reactions, and flow—so we can make better decisions about them. Therefore, we need more data, knowledge, expertise, and better decisions to succeed in optimizing our resources for digital transformation. That sends us right back to the point of leadership roles and our human factors and potential.

SUMMARY

As a digital transformation leader, becoming more should be your first commitment, even before you think about the transformative vision. Shift your focus to self-improvement, switching your mindset to possibility and positivity. Have the courage to face your fears, your emotions, and your limits, and acknowledge them before letting go of them. Take care of yourself to optimize your individual performance. Commit to your own personal transformation before expecting any change from others. You are responsible for yourself first.

Give yourself permission to leave your comfort zone, to explore your limits, to reach greater heights, and to feel your emotions. Even if the fear is paralyzing, like Nike says, "Just do it!" Do you feel like screaming from fear? Well, scream then. You may even laugh at yourself during the process, but go ahead and jump ahead to becoming more. Becoming more is the first link in the chain of change that leads to transformation.

Are you willing to make the essential commitment of becoming more? If yes, then start with the first action list below.

TAKING ACTIONS!

1. Identify some limiting beliefs you may have, and list them. List also negative emotions and feelings that you may have held on to (for example, any lack of self-confidence, the need to blame and not take responsibility, excessive ego, anger, resentment, the need to please others, frustration). Now set your mind to release them by practicing letting go. If they are too ingrained, set your intention to reprogram your brain with the opposite, positive beliefs and feelings.
2. Take a break, and shift your mind-set to positivity. Make a list of some outstanding, inspirational realizations others have made, regardless of their field of expertise or industry. Take a moment and focus on these achievements. Imagine the mind-sets of the leader(s) who realized them before you.
3. How is your physical health? What could you do to improve yourself, have more energy, increase your concentration, and unleash your intellectual capacities? Maybe you would benefit from improving your nutrition, exercising more, taking a vacation, and managing stress better. Find a way to improve your health by all means.
4. Decide that you are going to be more and commit yourself to being more regardless of the challenges you face. Write an agreement with yourself, and declare to yourself that you are going to rise above the challenges you will encounter while becoming more.
5. Now sign your declarations!

CHAPTER THREE

Visions That Transform

"Great leaders create more leaders, not followers. Great leaders have vision, share vision, and inspire others to create their own."

— *Roy T. Bennett,* The Light in the Heart

DEFINING YOUR VISION

If we are leading our people to individual transformation, we must show them the way by walking the path before them, instead of telling them where to go. To show them the way, we must first have a vision of it.

Although digital transformation requires great business understanding and skills, creating a digital transformation vision is not only a CXO's responsibility. Any leader should be able to create a vision for their team, organization, department, or business unit.

Many departments, projects, or services in your organization would perform even better if all their leaders could create and define a better vision for their entity. While digital transformation leaders who are leading a whole transformation would create the vision for the whole organization or business, transformational leaders within services, departments, and business units must create or develop the visions for their entities that align with their organization's main or corporate vision. These transformational leaders may or may not be part of the leadership team we spoke about in Chapter 1, but they are an extension of the top digital transformational leader.

Visionary leaders, wherever they are in their organizations, are well appreciated by top management for their capacity to extend the transformative vision at the different levels of their organization.

Transformative visions are created by genuine transformational leaders who see beyond what everyone else sees. Reading, understanding, and doing the actions in the first chapter will help digital transformation leaders create or extend the vision in a state of mind that favors positivity, possibility, and humanity.

The painful truth is that many organizations are led by leaders who are not committed, not convinced, and do not believe in their organization's vision. That may be because the vision does not offer possibilities for everyone involved or it lacks clarity. As a result, no matter what efforts are put into transforming the organization, frustration and negative outcomes emerge both within management and on the organizational sides. Then confusion, disengagement, and sometimes the feeling of being taken advantage of become negative barriers against transformation.

DEFINING THE VISION AT THE DIFFERENT LEVELS

Are you thinking that creating vision is for the executive level only? If so, let me show you otherwise with a personal story from early in my career.

After barely one year of experience in the marketplace, I was working as a technology-support analyst in a financial company. It was my second job. I worked in a department where we were supporting an application, managing it, developing it, and providing access to it for everyone in the company who worked on a computer. At first, I started out alone, but then another analyst was necessary. We were just two people doing the job, and it was exhausting. Daily, we had a queue of people from our office all the way down the main hall (mostly people who had recently started working or who had change positions). It was all about access and authorization. Many were upset that their access had not already been granted since they had already provided several documents or signatures when they had come earlier. We also had a long queue of different requests online from people already using the software. Then there were two phones that would not stop ringing with even more requests.

My colleagues and I who shared the open room/work platform formed the team that developed and supported all the new releases of the CRM (Customer Relationship Management) software. We had a new release every trimester. In addition, we managed query for another large database using query software. We were supporting Mac and PC users, and each used a different process.

After a trimester working like a crazy head who was supporting the entire department, I could map all the processes, types of requests, and analytical work we did. It became obvious to me that the department's services could be done better and that I could deliver a better service quality than what was expected from me. I had a greater vision for the service.

My vision was of a more efficient software-support service. I set the following goals for this more efficient service:

- To reduce the delay in the service we provided, especially for new account creation and query management.
- For managers to know what they should do and to provide for new employees upon their arrival.
- For new employees to know when and where to collect the information that would allow them to start working.
- For employees to find information about new software-function releases, important dates, known problems, and work-around solutions without having to call or stand in line, wasting precious time.
- To be more available for helping with functional and technical problems that truly required our analytical skill.

In fact, I was a bit surprised that in such a global and renowned organization there was such a mess. With my limited professional experience, I expected better from that famous organization. Being a junior in the workplace with less than three years of experience, I hesitated to propose my better vision to the management. However, I looked around me and said to myself, "Well, they hired me for this job. That means they believe in me. They believe I can deliver an adequate solution. So this is my challenge, and I am going to help them do a better job."

Easter break was just around the corner, and during Easter break, most parents take vacation, so the service would be less busy. I made an agreement with one of my colleagues. He would manage the service alone for the week of Easter break and the following week.

Meanwhile, I would work uninterruptedly on creating the new vision I had for the service and its new effectiveness.

During that week, I worked intensively and did the following:

1. Defined new business and service procedures and policies.
2. Wrote several communications to be automatically sent to different audiences at specific times.
3. Created intranet service pages for the service where I hosted the procedures and communications.
4. Created a "knowledge base" on the intranet, where I uploaded many "how-to" tutorials for known problems and work-arounds, including software-release management information and other types of precious information for managers, newcomers, and anyone who could use the department's services.
5. Wrote and sent out new communications to the whole organization about the new approach for service delivery in the department.

After two weeks of designing and implementing the new vision, we had a completely new service. As a result of this transformation, after those two weeks, the queue to our office had disappeared and was never to be seen again. The accounts creation and modification was done smoothly and quickly because the endless scouting for the right information and the right signatures was eliminated. The phone only rang randomly. People knew to go on the intranet site to find the information they needed. We had created a plan regarding what to communicate and the frequency of those communications. We kept it up to date.

As a result, we finally had time to focus on the backlog of database queries and could better support the application-development team in their preparation of new releases.

Everyone was served professionally and smoothly, and they could work efficiently as a result. There were no more complaints, just applause and thank-yous! My colleague and I had time to go to lunch at noon, leave on time for other things in our life after work, and talk with our colleagues while being in control of our work.

The head of our department was so impressed that he wanted to hire me directly—however, the consultancy company I worked for would not let happen due to their legal contract.

That was almost two decades ago and before digital transformation. But it illustrates that whatever level you are at, you can develop a vision to improve things and contribute to the organization's main vision. I did not have any authority; I was merely a junior software analyst with little experience. But I impacted the service and the work of many departments in the organization with my vision of a more efficient service unit.

I did not have the knowledge to do it right away, but I figured it out during the process. I did not let my limited years of experience or what people might think of my proposition prevent me from taking a stand for my new vision of service efficiency. The changes meant I would have less work to do in the future, but I did not care and was not afraid of being let go. I am not a position holder. As a consultant, I am a problem solver and a solution provider. I wanted to learn, deliver, grow, and then move on to the next phase of my career.

If I could make such an impact while I working as a junior analyst, barely out of school and with no leadership or managerial position, think what an impact you can make at your level with your leadership, management, or executive role. What can you change in your organization, service, department, or unit that will transform it and the people you serve? Take some time to visualize it!

THE VISION MUST BE ENGAGING

Top management vision is the most important vision. Many companies are spending vast sums of money to help get people "engaged" and improve processes and technology. Many of these efforts have a poor return on investment—costs skyrocket while ROI is minimal or negative. Could it be they need to review their approach and consider a transformation? Are they just fixing the symptoms, while the real problem is at the top of the organization, department, or unit?

The questions are, what should people be engaged in building? What should they commit to? Often the organization needs to answer these questions first to clarify the vision. This would help address the real issues and save the cost of executing projects that fail because they compete with each other or because they do not lead to real improvement. Digital transformation offers the opportunity to create or redefine organizations and business visions. This is your opportunity to define or contribute to that vision.

People do not become engaged with a vision that does not clearly show the benefits and the new environment it will create. They may not see the possibilities and opportunities in change, even when the new vision is presented. It may be that they are not prepared yet for the new transformation and only see what they are leaving behind. Remember that change brings disruption and emotional stress.

Besides clarifying the transformation for your people, go farther in helping them see the new possibilities and opportunities for them. Still, some may not be ready to appreciate a transformed environment, but be assured that the change process will help them grow to that level. Give them time, and allow them to understand that no one is to blame, that growth is a normal part of life.

Leaders must take time not just to define the vision to show how the environment has changed but to identify possible opportunities for their followers. They also need to enlighten their followers about why they must implement digital transformation and what would happen if they don't.

Digital transformation changes should be seen and thought of as a way of growing and becoming more, achieving more, and moving to the next season of the organization's or business' life.

Too often, leaders get stuck describing negative outcomes that cause change and neglect to identify the extra work needed to define the possibilities and then the opportunities that will result from the change.

Maybe that "marvelous" digital transformation will reduce the headcount in a department and replace the staff with a system. If that's how the change is communicated, even if it will reduce human error, there is nothing attractive about it for stakeholders in that department. As a result, they are not going to engage in such a change. They will worry about losing their position. In fact, they have been served a negative prediction about the upcoming change, instead of being given a clear vision for the company's future.

Here are a few questions that will help you define your vision:

- Who will be affected by the vision?
- What's in the vision for these people?
- Which new realities and professions are being created?
- What skills will still be needed in the organization?
- What other market opportunities will arise with such a transformation?

Where many leaders and organizations fail in getting engagement for the vision is in identifying new possibilities. As a leader, before you announce that one door is closing, you must identify new possibilities for development and help your people grow and realize that another door has opened.

It is normal for people to resist learning new things or doing things differently, but it is a whole new story when there is nothing in sight for them except layoffs or becoming obsolete, especially if they have been around for many years. The message they are getting is that the organization they've worked for is not built to last. It is not evolving and helping them grow for their next season in life. It is not inviting them to be more and have more, but will instead let them down, without even a dash of hope.

Digital transformation leaders must get a deeper understanding of the business they are in, what it is evolving toward, and which new innovations they can create or build around for their transformation vision. They must develop ways to inspire, adjust, and help people shift their mind-set toward the new vision. That is part of the digital transformation leader's commitment to rise above the challenges. Creating the new vision may require innovation, personal transformation, and so on, but the true leader is someone who can focus and see what can be achieved.

Some leaders may not have new opportunities to offer employees who are being let go. However, through their vision, they may inspire these employees to create new visions to serve the world in the next season of their lives. A digital transformation leader may inspire a redundant employee so much with their vision that the redundant employee successfully starts their own business, delivering new, innovative solutions and may even become a valuable supplier to their former employer. The redundant employee's knowledge of their former company can be a strong competitive advantage.

ELEMENTS OF THE DIGITAL VISION

1. User experience: how you interact and gather information from users and other parties and use it effectively for the following business phases:
    - marketing and communication
    - product development
    - value delivery method
    - customer service
    - partner relationships
2. Data science and business intelligence
3. Innovation and competition
4. Transformational leadership
5. The digitally enabled organization

VISIONING IS DONE WITH THE MIND

Brain science reveals that we don't see with our eyes. We see with our brain and through our eyes. The visionary sees what can be.

Never underestimate the work of a transformational leader sitting at their desk and appearing to do nothing valuable. The visioning work is done silently and in the mind. Creating a vision is done using two of the most powerful functions of the brain, according to the latest scientific discoveries in brain science:

1. Visualizing: using our brain to see what can be
2. Broadcasting: emitting and receiving information in the quantum field or atmosphere with our brain

This is one of the reasons I said in the introduction that you can take this book everywhere, whether you're on vacation or in bed.

Why Use Brain Science For Transformation

Transmiting and receiving station

We transmit and receive information at all time. Creation of our individual program.

Vision

We see with our brain first and through our eyes.

Memories

Conscious and subconscious mind

Conscious mind - short term memory/ subconscious mind - long term memory processing

- Then search and match our most focused visions.

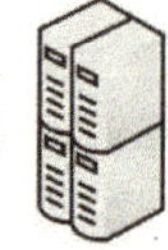

Messages

Send warning message of vision materializing.

Emotions

Reacting (Fear) versus responding to messages

Overprotective and Detective

Defensive job, scouting out for negativities or threats to protect us from, therefore, negative by default.

Dream or Reality?

The brain does not make any difference

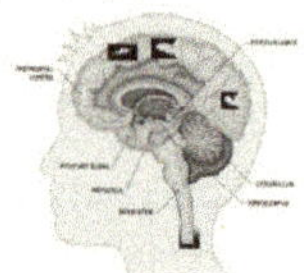

We can train our brain to achieve what we want: TRANSFORMATION!

Transformation and developing leadership skills can happen anywhere, not just the office. Being transformed and becoming more is a lifestyle!

Creating a transformative vision is smart work to do, and daydreaming is part of it. That's because we see with our brain and through our eyes.

CLARIFYING YOUR VISION

A Guideline to Creating and Clarifying Your Vision

The following approach applies, whether it is a large organization or a small team, department, or a project vision.

1. Today's Situation

What is the business we are in and our situation today (in relation to the digital transformation taking place)? This is like the caterpillar in nature before it turns into a butterfly in the next life season.

2. Evolutions for Tomorrow

As in the above analogy, how the nature of your business will evolve or change. What is being changed in the marketplace for the business you are in, and what will it look like in one to five years (what are the possibilities)? How is the business being reinvented or evolving (processes, production, delivery, etc.)? If we don't do anything, what will happen? What is the market evolving toward?

3. Opportunities

What opportunities will be there in the newly evolved environment? What opportunities can we take from that change for (1) the organization and (2) the people in the organization?

4. Propositions for *now*

The caterpillar starts its transformation today so it can take advantage of tomorrow's new environment. Where are we now? What can we start doing from where we are now? What are the next steps, or first few steps, we can take now? How can we prepare for the transformation?

4 Steps To Define and Clarify Your Organization Vision

1 Define Today's Situation
Current situation

2 Evolutions Foreseen for Tomorrow
possibilities

3 Opportunities for Tomorrow

4 What We Can Do Now

The Digital Transformation Success Formula
www.digitaltransformationleaders.com

SUMMARY

A clear vision is very important for you, the leader, and for your organization. More than that, the vision should be transformative. A transformative vision will take you to another level of performance and living a different experience. When creating your vision, take time away to clear your mind. Unleash your mind; let go of resentment and negative experiences in your present to focus mainly and exclusively on your vision and making it transformative. See your vision in your mind; feel it, experience it, and write it down clearly.

TAKING ACTIONS!

Develop your vision by doing the exercise above in defining and clarifying your vision. You should have at least the following points:

1. Describe the business you are in and what it is evolving into.
2. Describe your new market and changes the business will evolve into in the next five-plus years (possibilities).
3. List at least five new, innovative opportunities for your business to fill and profit from in the new market.
4. Name one thing you can transform to improve efficiency in your organization, department, service, or unit.
5. Name your stakeholders who the transformative vision will serve or effect, and how they will each benefit from the new vision.
6. Describe how different groups of people can support the vision at different levels to make it a reality.
7. Create or redraft your vision using the information above to make it appealing to your stakeholders.

CHAPTER FOUR

Turning Your Vision Into A Mission

Once you have a mission, you can't go back to having a job.

— SHAI AGASSI

A transformative vision feels great when thinking of the improvements and transformations it could make possible for others. Consider how people and their interests are represented within the vision, and how we make that vision happen. That is what we are going to explore next.

Before transformation can take place and the vision can be achieved, we need to engage dedicated people prepared for a mission. The mission is to create the transformation for us and others. Therefore, turning the vision into a mission will multiply the chances of it becoming a reality.

A mission is the "why" that keeps us moving and overcoming obstacles even when we don't feel like it. It is the binding agreement we make with ourselves. Its power overcomes any written agreement we could have signed.

A mission gives your "partners in crime" the drive to overcome personal conflicts, internal doubts and fears, limiting beliefs, and any other challenges. This is because the drive created by their purpose overcomes any obstacles that may otherwise limit them physically, mentally, professionally, or personally. With a great mission, you can easily create missionaries who will work day to day knowing their small part contributes to building the transformation and is an important and purposeful assignment in a grand vision.

For the visionary leader, a mission also reminds them of the responsibilities they have to lead people according to each individual's purpose. This is the secret for gaining loyalty, commitment, and getting the best from people. By acknowledging people's purpose and motivation, you directly tap into their biggest reservoir of strength and greatness. At the same time, you allow the ones who do not resonate with the mission and vision to intentionally walk away toward their own mission.

There is nothing negative about people walking away from an organization when they are not aligned. In fact, it is best for both parties when people choose to walk away from an organization after a clear vision and mission were well communicated and understood. This will prevent unnecessary conflicts and resistance and will save the costs in aligning IT and business functions.

DEVELOPING MISSIONARIES

A mission is the "why" that keeps us moving and overcoming obstacles even when we don't feel like it. Still, it is not enough to have a mission; you must develop missionaries for it. Many powerful visions not only reveal the mission but also prompt people to become missionaries themselves, in hopes of participating in a powerful vision.

One example I can think of is the following vision statement from the vice president and prime minister of the United Arab Emirates (UAE) and emir of Dubai, H.H. Sheikh Mohammed bin Rashid Al Maktoum, as written on his LinkedIn profile (at the time of writing this book's first edition): "We are building a new reality for our people, a new future for our children, and a new model of development."

The vision statement above expresses both a vision and a mission for the UAE and Dubai. It inspires every (political) leader in that country to find out more about that vision and be part of such a powerful mission. It is a mission that is even worth competing for. It is one that speaks to their people's hearts, souls, and purpose. It is a statement made to call on leaders and missionaries. Furthermore, it is a vision statement that calls for people of that nation to trust in their leader's vision and mission, a major point that I will discuss later.

In the next chapter, I will explain how to announce your vision in a way that will call people to become missionaries and engage/collaborate in making the vision a reality. There are leadership techniques you can use to call on these leaders and missionaries wherever they are in the organization, even if their leadership qualities are currently asleep. These techniques are facilitated by digital technology.

STARTING A "MISSIONARY FIRE" IN YOUR ORGANIZATION

Do you know that many people are actually bored, unfulfilled, and hoping to have a great leader appear to help them uncover their purpose and turn them into excited missionaries? As a digital transformation leader, you will need to create your support team by calling on and choosing among great leaders who share your vision, your standards, and your mission to transform your organization or business.

When a leader helps you uncover or follow your purpose, you remain loyal to that leader and the purpose in general. Disengagement is less likely; rather, you will seek a higher level of involvement.

Now there is something that many leaders are afraid of which is seldom spoken about openly—it is the insecurity that a leader may feel about working with someone who is highly involved, expressing their own leadership qualities, and who may thus be more competent in one aspect or another than the leader.

I believe in the saying, "Hire people who are more knowledgeable than you." It is because they help you reach an even higher level of achievement. You shouldn't feel intimidated if someone working for you is more competent than you in a given area.

There are plenty of personality types, people with personal agendas, etc. who are worth worrying about but skill and competence are good things. Above all, you are looking for integrity from your support team, nothing less. We will speak about building a support team in the next chapter.

That said, as you are preparing for your missionaries, make the level of performance you have established for the organization and its leaders, be reflected in the mission. Do this before you choose your team leaders.

DEFINING THE STANDARDS FOR YOUR MISSIONARIES

You should define the standards, performance level, and company culture for your missionaries. In general, *A*-level leaders will hire other *A*-level leaders. A-level leaders have higher standards, and they are either secure or less insecure than most. *A*-level leaders function like a top-level sports team, and they value winning as a team much more than flexing their egos in the mirror. They are driven by a desire to transform things for the better and leave an admirable legacy for humanity.

B-level leaders will often avoid hiring *A*-level leaders because *B*-level leaders generally don't want to eclipsed by an A-level leader. *B*-level leaders hire *B*- and *C*-level leaders as a rule. They are more comfortable with an under-performing team than with an *A*-level leader who is seen as more effective than them. There will always be more conflict in this type of team than among strictly *A*-level leaders.

You must be clear about the type of company culture, standards, and levels of performance you want to establish and choose your missionaries accordingly. I remember reading once that, "You don't hire people to train them to be successful. You hire successful people."

In this context, you will have to define *successful* as it relates to your business or organization's mission and ensure that you match the missionaries with it. For example, if your mission is about, let's say, helping people by problem solving, then you want missionaries or team leaders who are known problem solvers. This is why, again, it's important to define your mission and define the type of missionaries you want before recruiting them. This is ultimately part of building your business, organization, or team culture.

SUMMARY

In summary, it's about developing a transformative mission and then engaging your missionaries in their responsibilities, behaviors, and commitment to the cause. This is the backbone of the company culture, from which the rest of the company culture may then be developed.

TAKING ACTIONS!

Here are the steps for turning the vision into a mission and creating missionaries who will embrace, commit to, build, defend, and live by that mission.

1. Define your *why*.
2. Identify your winners—who will benefit? List the possible benefits.
3. Define the consequences of doing nothing? What are the possible ramifications for everyone involved?
4. Create a brief strategy. How can the transformation be accomplished?
5. Identify top missionaries (leaders) and all possible support staff (valuable for creating your support team later). Who can come together to make the transformation happen?

6. List at least the top five organizational values you want to create.
7. Prepare your documents, your speeches, proposals, and anything else needed to create your mission and get new missionaries (transformation-support leaders) using the information gathered above.

CHAPTER FIVE

Announcing to Engage

He who does not trust enough, will not be trusted.
— *Lao Tzu*

PREPARING YOUR PEOPLE TO FLY

Transformational leaders are bearers of positive messages but still, they must earn trust. You'll be preparing people to fly with your vision while preventing disengagement. Once your vision is ready, you need to prepare people to receive your communications and get engaged in the transformation process. Do not announce it directly to people without preparing them to receive your message first. They may not be hungry for it and may not care. It is too easy for them to resist leaving their comfort zone. It is easier for them to create barriers, walls, or distance instead. You want more from them, and I am going to show you how to get more from them and yourself. You may be well into planning and executing your vision. *But, in fact, this is the team's first step in the transformation process, and it's a very important one.* If you don't properly introduce the mission, you will meet more resistance, challenges, and roadblocks later.

Don't skip this step!

It is wonderful to have a great vision, whether you created it or inherited it. You may feel highly empowered with a mandate to carry out a great vision, but you may also be scared by such a challenge and its responsibilities, knowing that the outcome depends on so many other people. Maybe you think you have a small, medium, or limited role in the organization. But don't get discouraged, because you will be leading a team and not forcing them. And you know what? Your organization needs your leadership.

People need a better vision and would easily say yes to any vision that would bring them positive transformation, transformation that would spread to every area of their lives right away. Keep that in mind. What they don't want is uncertainty. They want immediate gratification, as discussed in Chapter 2 Uncertainty creates fear, and fear causes failure in both individuals and organizations.

People fear losing what they already have or working too hard for too little. They also fear change in their daily routine and resist change unless they see the reward for doing so right before them. As we discussed in Chapter 2, people want immediate gratification. Statistics about failed IT projects indicate there must be a better way to lead change and transformation projects.

Don't let people pull you into their storm. Pull them into your peace.
—Sarah Carswell

TAMING THE FEAR FACTOR IN PEOPLE

Let's refer again to the latest discoveries in brain science, looking at neuroplasticity to teach us about our fears. Fear is an emotion, and neuroscientists can now see it in the brain. Fear comes from the memory of anything painful or uncomfortable that our brain has registered before. Whenever we risk going out of our comfort zones, our brain quickly retrieves a negative, fear-based emotion to warn us of something unfamiliar, bad, or painful that may happen. Because of that, fear is not real but just an old memory.

When confronted with fear, we need to bring our mind to the present moment and validate with our conscious mind that what we fear does not exist at the moment and not in the future, either. In fact, you can create the future. This is an opportunity to reprogram the brain with the proper goals, mission, and future vision and to use our energy to create what we want for that future using faith. In other words, it is important to address fear, increase faith, and focus on the present moment to create the new, transformed future.

Fears can be expressed in many forms: aggressiveness, defensiveness, withdrawal, manipulation, ego wars, overly controlling behaviors, and so on.

Communicating your vision will not go well unless you address the fear factor. In fact, I believe this is another way to implement change successfully—by addressing the fear factor from several angles.

Many organizations hold company-wide meeting where they reveal upcoming changes, new leadership, or reorganization plans. Before the meeting even starts, employees start chatting and worrying, with rumors spreading through the grapevine. By the time the meeting is held, tension has already built and continues growing after the meeting ends causing additional worries, resistance, and so forth. People start imagining where they fit into the new plan.

Some people are such natural worriers that even if a positive change is announced, they focus on the hidden "bad news" under it, and they let their fears guide them. Often, they rally more people behind their fears and build a wall of resistance that executives and leaders never predicted.

Even people who are not naturally worriers may start wondering why there is so much fuss over digital transformation and whether it is necessary. Why should they give up their old systems, their old processes, or their old ways of working? Can they just move on without all these changes? They may even think of the digital transformation leader, CIO, or director as someone who is just looking to establish their presence and that digital transformation is not necessary. This is especially true when company profits are already high and team members don't see the need for digital transformation or any other change.

Though some employees may be happy, possibly getting promoted or placed in a new position, maybe with a salary increase, they can quickly be demotivated. Their happiness may be short-lived. Early rewards may not be enough to motivate them on a long-term basis, keeping them engaged in the full implementation of digital transformation.

Basically, you need to prepare people to carry the change process through to completion, even if they are onboard early, so when their strength, loyalty, and adaptability are put to the test, they will remain engaged and active.

If separation is needed, it is not always bad because change is an occasion to realign and move to the next chapter of life. But you want it to happen early because it costs less. Decisive individuals may choose to resign, especially when they have other choices or are sure of what they want and that what they want is not in line with the organization's vision.

Your communication about the organization's vision should be clear enough to allow people to make the choice to stay or leave. Communicate to win followers and weed out those whose mission is not in line with your organization or business.

Disengagement, on the other hand, is a complete loss both for the individual and the organization. Disengagement indicates one or more of the following is happening: confusion, nonalignment, lack of trust, lack of interest, fear, and/or lack of leadership. You want to avoid that.

Healing fear can be done by using the power of the brain, thinking ahead to acknowledge and shatter fears, then using self-compassion to heal from them. You and everyone else deserves better than living in fear. Invite and encourage your people to shatter and heal from their personal fears. However, success depends completely on each individual. Remember, no one wants to feel vulnerable. It takes a strong and emotionally intelligent person to face their vulnerabilities. To increase engagement and overcome fear, start with yourself—right now, using the following infographic. Lead by example. "Monkey see, monkey do."

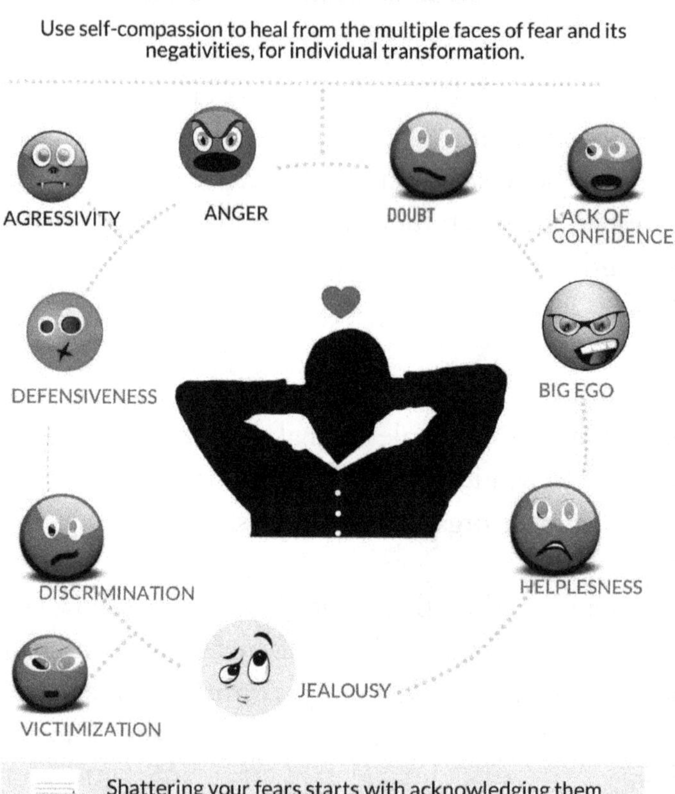

A CLOSER LOOK AT DISENGAGEMENT

People disengage for many reasons, but whatever the reason(s) might be, one thing is true: the organization and its people are not aligned. I am not speaking about superficial alignment. Rather, disengagement is an individual behavior before it becomes true for a group. Therefore, individual consideration is necessary to turn around disengagement. As with most things, prevention is better than reaction. It is cheaper and saves time—many people's sanity.

A disengaged employee is not a disengaged person. Disengagement indicates commitment to the vision or mission is lacking. Let's see an example of disengagement with two different employees. The first person is Pat, an employee who shows up, does their time, and stays busy, though their quality level may be below expectations. The second person is Avery, who simply hates being constantly busy and is unproductive due to a lack of vision and strategy (we'll talk more about Avery in a moment).

Both Pat and Avery do just enough to keep their jobs and collect a paycheck, but they lack trust and interest in what they are doing. If they find better jobs that also add more meaning to their lives, they will happily move on.

Pat is bored and regularly discusses searching for another job at home. Pat is not a disengaged person. In fact, Pat is committed to family and shows up to work just to support them. Pat is disengaged with the company and where it is going. If Pat was disengaged because of the pay only, Pat would work harder or learn something new and seek a promotion (unless Pat does not trust the company to give a promotion).

Or maybe Pat has just reached a career plateau and wants a change. Whatever the case may be, Pat is not a disengaged person; Pat is just not aligned with the company anymore. The right leadership and realignment may turn Pat into a better investment for the company. It would also make Pat happier.

Avery has been in the company for about twenty years. Avery started as an intern and has been promoted to several roles in various departments. Avery has seen a lot of changes in two decades and recognizes that there are opportunities within the company. Avery is emotionally attached to the company and is not looking to leave. But Avery is miserable at work. Avery has worked in several departments and feels that it's the same in each.

Aver see that people lack information about where the company is heading. Communications over the last few years have often been contradictory, and with all the market changes, multiple change implementations, and changes in the CEOs and CIOs, it is confusing. It is often difficult to know who is responsible for what and where to find support for daily activities. As a result, Avery has lost trust both in the company and its management. Avery has lost confidence in the future of the company. However, Avery does not have the personal strength to leave—too afraid of starting anew somewhere else. The job is necessary to maintaining a comfortable lifestyle. The job provides a good position with prestige, medical insurance, and a nice company car, and Avery owns a house close to the workplace and definitely wants to stay there. Avery has a great relationship with colleagues, and some of them are close friends. Avery loves the work and does it well, but is still unproductive. Avery's work often goes unused, even though it is top quality. The bottleneck comes from top management and affects decision-making, causing Avery to redo everything again and again, just like turning in circles.

While Avery loves aspects of the work, and is in no way a disengaged person, all the turmoil and indecision from above causes disengagement and disbelief. Avery is not in position to change the status quo of the organization.

Though the organization may be coping fine in the market place, it is not as good as it used to be. Avery keeps hoping that the next change will be the one that will transform the company, but is getting tired of the situation. This causes impatience and disengagement with others. Conflicts arise often as a result, which also affects Avery's personal life. The whole situation undermines Avery's personal well-being. Disengaging from the job is a form of protection. Avery is not a disengaged person but an employee who is disengaged with the ongoing changes at the company.

If nothing is done, Avery may become a bad investment for the company in the long term. Avery is not likely to leave the company but is disengaging more and more. If proper leadership provided meaningful engagement, Avery could become a greater investment for the company and be a happier person.

Now, my question for you is, how are you engaging your people, team, and followers in the workplace? Think about it for a few seconds.

You cannot engage people using regular job-related work. These are just tasks, and people do not stay engaged long by doing tasks—not even the ones they love doing.

Soon such tasks become repetitive and boring, and team members will reach a plateau and ask, "Now what?" People engage with a vision of a greater tomorrow and commit to the mission of creating that vision. The vision taps into their energy and encourages them to keep working toward that goal in their current position or elsewhere in the organization. This is what you want. A great vision is what you need to gain engagement, and engaging people is a two-way thing. Engagement is measured in the quality of the mission and vision and in the way they are communicated.

PREVENTING DISENGAGEMENT

Preventing disengagement starts with creating and then announcing the vision. Previously, I led you to create an irresistible and transformative vision. Now, understand that no matter how irresistible the vision may be, it will not come to reality overnight or by itself. We need missionaries to realize that vision, and we need them to want it as much as, if not more than, we, the digital transformation leaders and top management, do. Therefore, we need to build the energy—create the hunger—for making that vision a reality during the *announcement* phase. Here we go!

THE FOUR STEPS OF THE ANNOUNCE TO ENGAGE PHASE

1. Prepare the first change announcement.
2. First communication—announce the market change and create a sense of urgency for a transformation.
3. Build the leadership-support team.
4. Second communication—announce the upcoming transformation and the support team.

The announcement phase in its entirety is not covered in this chapter only, but it started with the preparation in the previous chapters and continues into the following chapters.

STEP 1: PREPARING THE FIRST CHANGE ANNOUNCEMENT

The first step, preparing the first change announcement, requires the leader to do some preparatory work as suggested in the previous chapters.

- start self-transformation
- create the vision
- prepare the mission

STEP 2: ANNOUNCING THE SITUATION AND CREATING THE URGENCY (FIRST ANNOUNCEMENT)

The first communication is about informing the organization about the changes in the marketplace in order to create urgency. Nothing should be mentioned about the business or organizational changes or specific vision at this stage. However, the organization should be assured that management is working on defining and adopting the best strategy to maintain and improve its position. This is very important.

The goal of this first communication is to remove blame, create urgency, and pre-engage employees in transforming their organization. Organizations where people are fed change after being made hungry for change will experience fewer struggles. Good communication will result in employees developing a hunger for the transformation.

Creating hunger in employees develops loyalty, informs their purpose, prevents disengagement, and creates involvement in the transformation before it begins. This is like an invitation to join forces with the leader/captain. It flatters people by recognizing what they contribute to the organization. It speaks to their purpose.

After this announcement, top management or the announcer will be watched more closely. This is the most important time to lead by example. What was said must be respected and in line with leaders' actions. It is a time when people's minds are being shifted. It is a transition time before the next announcement.

Those who are aligned with the company and loyal to it step forward.

These leaders will come forward to offer their contributions and propositions. Those who are not aligned with the company start looking in other directions. To make the best of this period, you can launch, for example, a call for innovative ideas about what the company can do to adjust to the digital transformation.

Make it fun and easy, while starting to transform your people by using digital technologies. Digital technology brings everyone closer and allows us to express our emotions live through the use of social media, The Internet of Things, our smartphones, and mobility. During the announcement phase, launch a mobile application and a transformation-contribution campaign to start engaging the organization.

You can even extend the invitation to your customers with a mobile application and engage everyone in the transformation. The advantage with digital transformation is that the ways of taking advantage of it are limited only by your imagination. Why not tap into more resources for the transformation? Remember from Chapter 2, that digital transformation leaders must optimize their resources. You are doing just that!

STEP 3: BUILDING THE LEADERSHIP SUPPORT TEAM

Though this step officially designates the people on the support team, it does not start there; it began with creating the mission charter. Step 3 helps refine the charter by identifying leaders who want to engage in the transformation by being proactive and the ones who appear to be stepping aside, frozen, or disengaged. I'll show you how to choose your transformation leadership team in Chapter 6.

STEP 4: ANNOUNCING THE UPCOMING TRANSFORMATION AND SUPPORT TEAM (SECOND ANNOUNCEMENT)

When the organization's vision and high-end strategy is revealed and the support team is introduced, organizational restructuring begins to take place. People, departments, and teams are assigned new leaders, and support is created for the implementation ahead.

In both step 1 and step 4, the following will be of utter importance for the digital transformation's success.

ARE YOU TRUSTWORTHY?

This is the question your audience will be asking themselves as you take the lead in announcing change. They will not give you their trust freely—you need to earn it. Whatever you say or do, they will ask themselves whether they can trust you. This is, of course, a fear-based reaction.

Your team's trust in you or your proposition, in fact, is rather a perception shaped by their existing opinions of you. But now, during your presentation, you have another opportunity to inspire them and earn their trust. It is time to *show* them what you have in store for them; they will decide to follow you or not.

This presentation is your opportunity to demonstrate the following:

- Experience: you know what you are talking about—without the "I know it all" attitude.
- Caring: you care about their future and that of the organization.
- Confidence: you believe in what you are saying, in the vision, in yourself, and in them without an off-putting excessive ego.

- Consistency: what you said last time and what you have been doing is consistent with what you are telling them this time—or else provide specific explanations.
- Openness: you will be collaborating with other leaders and listening to employees' ideas and concerns, even if you choose not to implement them.
- Professionalism: they want to see a leader and one who did their homework!
- Integrity: they want to know that their leader is trustworthy at all times.

You can show them all the above things in your presentation, starting with your positive body language, the inspiring words you choose, how you listen to and answer their questions, who you choose for your leadership support team, and the interactions you have with them.

You can find a book on effective communication to help you. But know that when the floor is yours, your body language and the tone of your voice will speak louder than your words themselves. You must speak to your people's unspoken fears.

TAKING ADVANTAGE OF NEUROPLASTICITY

Brain-science offers solutions for better communication. Neuroplasticity offers us the ability to adjust and embrace change successfully.

Neuroplasticity is one of the latest discoveries in brain science. It says that our brain is capable of developing new neural pathways as we train it to throughout our lifetime. It means something quite contrary to the popular belief that you cannot teach an old dog new tricks. Science proves that you can!

With neuroplasticity, beliefs, thoughts, and emotions can be seen in the brain along with their effects, whether positive or negative. Here is some key information learned from the latest brain-science studies, information that changes almost everything we know about our brain capacity and how we can achieve more success.

This is what will help us improve our communication:

- Use short, concise sentences with a maximum of ten (10) words, as our brain can keep only a limited number of words in consciousness at one time.
- Allow people a few seconds to better assimilate the information before moving on.
- Think about creating a more receptive, less stressful atmosphere before communicating your vision—stressful people are less receptive.

This is an element of the second part of the announcement, where the leader(s) have prepared and are ready (almost) to announce who they have picked to navigate the changing environment, the direction they are taking, and the leaders supporting these changes.

After the first announcement, allow at least two weeks before the next announcement. Consider a period between two weeks and three months, depending on your organization's size and the logistics of company-wide meetings. The time will be useful in creating urgency, shifting mindsets, and unleashing your people's creativity and transformative power. Potential leaders for the transformational-leadership support team will be revealed or confirmed during this period, as well.

In the meantime, put your efforts into building the support team and developing the strategic plan. After gathering and analyzing much information from the urgency creation phase, be it two weeks or a month, start the next phase, which is announcing the change and introducing the support team. I call that second announcement, "getting people engaged by feeding their hunger." But before you can successfully feed their hunger, gather information from the team and others to help flavor the food to their tastes. Launch a type of transformation-participation contest.

SUMMARY

In times of transformation, people are waiting to be addressed, oriented, and even reassured. Reassuring them does not mean providing them with the solutions. Sometimes, the best reassurance may be knowing that we are in this together and that a leader thought about them and has a plan to help figure out things. Even better than that, knowing they are included in the plan, counted on, understood, and supported through it all will create an atmosphere of engagement and trust. As much as you need your people's engagement, they need your communication and your guidance. Don't leave them in the dark alone; communicate empathetically with them, and they will engage in creating your business vision or the best vision for themselves.

TAKING ACTIONS!

1. Use the "Healing from Fears" infographic and acknowledge your fears in all their forms (listed or not). Then, using self-compassion, shatter these fears, for they are not real. On the other hand, they are real obstacles to your advancement.
2. Write down the opposite emotions of your fears and practice feeling them. Remember, the brain does not recognize any

difference between what is real and what is not, so you have control over the emotions you feel. Choose to feel positive emotions and heal yourself.

3. Prepare the announcement by completing the following steps.

Step 1. From the actions in chapters one and two, consider the changes, the stakeholders, and the employees involved. What are some fears you can anticipate from people?

Don't hesitate to ask people.

Step 2. Are these fears real? What are they based on?

Step 3. How can you address these fears? (Remember to use the opportunities to offset the fears.)

Step 4. How can you reassure people?

Step 5. Have a mobile application developed for your company with some interactive functions that allow you to interact with employees (and customers) using social media and mobility. Design a strategic and fun campaign your employees, contractors, and customers can use to suggest innovative ideas and express points of view to enhance the organization's business and fulfill customer wishes in the digital era.

Prepare a digital transformation participation poll or contest to involve your people and gather information from them. You can get help from marketing, customer service, and human resources to design an appropriate campaign.

You can also create a campaign especially for your business or organization's leaders. That will help to provide you more information for building your leadership team. Be creative; give them a fun challenge to do with their team's support, and let them surprise you.

Step 6. Create your second announcement with the above info, including your vision and mission for the company. Include results from the interactive campaign, and show how your employees and customers are already taking part in creating a shared vision. Reward some of the best ideas in the campaign. To reduce fears, engage people, help switch mindsets, and unleash creativity, continue making the process fun. Introduce your transformation leadership team. Inspire people to trust these leaders, the vision, and the transformed future.

Step 7. If you did the campaign for customers, follow up and reward customers who participated.

CHAPTER SIX

Creating the Transformation Support Team

Don't fear failure. Fear being in the exact same place next year as you are today.

— UNKNOWN

It is the journey that brings us transformation, not the destination. In this chapter, we step back a little to the third step of the Announcing to Engage phase. It is just after the first announcement while preparing for the second. So far, you've been making your transformative vision attractive with different groups of people in mind. You have an inspiring mission waiting for missionaries to contribute to and execute. You've created urgency with your first announcement.

Now some leaders are developing the hunger to help and to participate in the transformation. You are receiving information live through the people participation in the campaign using the mobile application. Set time apart daily or weekly to evaluate the data you are receiving from the campaign.

Keep an eye and an ear open to identify the leaders who want to and can build the transformation with you. Create a set of criteria to qualify the leaders for your transformation-leadership team and continue to observe and evaluate them.

Your leadership team is going to be like your wings or your extended self and the main executors of your plan. This group is of capital importance because they can help you realize your vision or block it. As such, this group must be created carefully and strategically based on some proven rules.

The leaders in your group are not meant to be copies of you, but a pool of varied and complementary skills, personas, and experiences that will harmoniously work together toward achieving the business or organization's vision.

No matter how varied, what the members must meet some shared requirements to fulfill their role in supporting the transformation.

They must:

- be faithful and loyal to the organization;
- believe in the transformative vision;
- have and demonstrate respect for each other;
- commit to the vision;
- have the right mind-set; and
- share some common interests.

For some large organizations, it sometimes takes years to create the right team who can successfully conduct change through completion. Team-building exercises and training are not enough to bind people together on a common mission. Going through real-life challenges, sharing personal experiences, and making critical decisions either creates the necessary bonds or simply causes the team to fall apart when the personalities clash.

Therefore, creating the right team is a process in itself. Adequate support from a neutral and specialized third party can be beneficial in building and sustaining that team. Continuously supporting the leadership team is a great strategic and long-term investment.

THE TRUTH ABOUT YOUR SUPPORT TEAM

As a leader, your support team is, after your brain, your most powerful resource. Building it is a major task, and it should not be rushed or you may lose precious time.

The best team is able to carry your vision forward, even when you are not available. Providing that you created a roadmap, empowered them, and created the right pool of competencies, skills, and personalities, your leadership team can help you drive the transformation. But a roadmap does not guarantee you will arrive at the expected destination. Your leadership team will, again, work with you to bypass obstacles, storms, dead ends, and you name it. Even if the final destination is modified along the way.

While each member of the team may have a different background or specialty, they all must believe in the vision and be able to work together in challenging situations. Team members must be people who know how to tame their egos to let the vision shine.

As simple as this may appear, an unfit team or one with too many ego wars will delay the transformation, if not kill it. In that case, as a leader, you will spend more time on conflict management and rework than progressing with the vision.

I have had the opportunity to implement change projects with several support teams. For the most productive teams I worked with, I attribute our success to:

- great teamwork
- great partnerships between people
- a shared mission
- trust, a shared level of performance and quality
- respect and appreciation

The most unproductive teams were challenged by:

- lack of trust
- conflict of interests (perceived or real)
- excessive egos
- lack of leadership
- randomly assigned teams
- unclear mission
- highly divided and guarded territories, where managers make their territories non-inclusive

Let's classify the leaders as levels *A*, *B*, and *C*, with *A* being the greatest. *A*-level leaders want to work with other *A*-level leaders, and they can form a powerful team where they support each other and maintain high standards. They will not have *B*-level or *C*-level leaders in top positions.

As mentioned before, *B*-level leaders will often avoid working with *A*-level leaders, as they may be worried the *A*-level leader will outshine them. Instead, they will choose other *B*-level and *C*-level leaders. In this organization of *B*-level and *C*-level leaders, you get more conflicts, more emotional turmoil, and a lower standard of work than you find with the *A*-level group.

PEOPLE WILL NOT GO AS FAST AS THEY CAN BUT WILL GO AT THE PACE OF THEIR LEADER

The leaders of the support group determine the standards and the company or business culture. The support team generally comes from middle management and downward.

With an *A*-level leader organization as the support group, implementation time is shorter, tolerance is better, and work standards are higher.

The biggest challenges to change implementation often come from middle management. Both top management and employees may suffer greatly.

As organizations become larger, more global, and more reactive, the use of the matrix-organization model becomes more common. Local executives are facing more challenges as they lose power or authority over their organization. The need for authentic and transformational leaders is, therefore, becoming more urgent and makes the difference between successful transformations and failed ones.

Carefully created and well guided leadership teams are more likely to succeed. Leadership teams accidently brought together or merely initiated but not fully trained to lead or that lack the necessary skills to do so will most likely fall apart during the transformation.

Accidental and merely initiated teams may have had only one or two teambuilding events at the start of the transformation. While this is a great initiative, it is not enough. Organizations need to have a growth plan that will last throughout the transformation. Digital transformation leadership teams need a growth journey, not a launch event to accomplish the transformation. The greatest challenges are ahead of them, and often these challenges require more people and soft skills than technology or business skills.

Choosing your support team is about maximizing your organization's success. As an example, here is a story of choosing my soccer team players as a kid.

When I was a child, my friends and I would play soccer. It was mainly the boys who played soccer between themselves, but occasionally, the girls would join in.

All of us loved to have Jimmy, who was my friend Louis' cousin, on our team, as he was a top player. I would do my best to have Louis, Robenson (my older brother), and Ginette (my older sister) on my team, and I'd let the other captain have Jimmy. They were always happy to have Jimmy because of his unmatched ability to shoot directly to the goal (we used to call him "uncle end-shooter"). But Jimmy had a weak point that made him unpredictable: Jimmy was too sensitive.

When upset Jimmy would cry terribly, and we sometimes had to wait until he finished to resume play. Sometimes, Jimmy even stormed away if he felt badly cheated, leaving us with one less team member. Jimmy used to let his emotions overshadow his abilities. Therefore, I would secure my best players and let go of Jimmy, whom I considered only second best.

We all knew Jimmy very well, and some of us would tap into Jimmy's weakest point to destabilize him if we felt it would help us win. Jimmy was not emotionally intelligent (yet). Therefore, I preferred to team with others.

Louis was the same age as me and a great player—I would say a better player than my brother Robenson who was just one year younger. When I had to choose between the two of them, I'd choose Louis. In that case, all family bonds were put aside, and I chose Louis over my brother because I wanted to win, and I chose the one who I believed gave me the best chance to win. I still loved my brother most; however, it was not about family but building a winning team.

The same must be applied when creating your transformation-leadership team. The goal is to lead and implement change successfully, and criteria such as family, friends, and protégés should not come first. Ability to lead, integrity, communication skills, experience, emotional intelligence, reliability, and leadership skills are the criteria that matter most for a successful transformation-leadership team.

EVERY TEAM NEEDS SOME PREPARATION

Even the ideal team needs some preparation. Once, I implemented a transformation project internationally with the support team members based in the UK and Belgium. It was about implementing a new project management approach to provide better quality deliverables after a merger and acquisition. I was based in Belgium in the company headquarters and led a team based in England.

On my first few trips, I could feel the resistance, as the employees of the company that was bought out were not happy changing everything and being monitored. After the first year, the employees were satisfied with the quality of their deliverables but not with the executives at the headquarters in Belgium. After my first visits, the employees complained to their local executives about me checking out their work and changing their processes, but their executives and the executives at the headquarters had tasked me with this mission.

The British executives acknowledged their employees' concerns, reassured them, and instilled in them the company's new vision and mission. I personally acknowledged their concerns and the transformation taking place. Though we were working virtually most of the time, we worked together as a great international team. As a result, in one year, we had turned the situation around and created a new project-delivery story, a story that both headquarters in Belgium and the organization in England were happy about.

THE ORGANIZATION THAT IS NOT READY FOR CHANGE AND TRANSFORMATION

Some organizations are not ready for change and even less ready for a transformation. One example was another buy-out of a historic and well-established company in two close European countries. Employees from each of these organizations just were not accepting each other as part of the same organization with the same goals. Beyond the business, it became more a matter of cultural affairs. The owner company was happy to exercise its power, going global and implementing its global strategy. But the middle management from the bought-out company did not want to accept any idea coming from the owner-company and would resist transformation. They wanted to keep part of their identity, and with that, their country's legacy.

Any change or transformation was met with massive resistance from most of middle management, whether openly or in a manipulative way. The company's headquarters then kept changing top management, in hopes of changing the mindset. They tried executives from both countries. But the middle-management wall was so strong and defensive it effectively stalled all transformation projects. That created a long history of projects that cost vast sums of money and achieved nothing.

The vision was not shared, and trust was nonexistent in that blended organization. The number of change projects was alarming, and often, they were not tied to one vision simply because each party seemed to have its own vision (official or not). After about ten years of continuous chaos, the parent company gave up and transferred most of their operations to other countries that offered both lower costs and acceptance of their leadership.

Maybe a big financial crisis would have helped create the urgency to change. But the organization was well established in their country, was doing well, and was a main economic pillar. As a result, they resisted all attempts from the headquarters to change.

There are also the organizations that overcome their greatest challenges and come together when their interests are at stake. I was happy to work for an organization like this. My greatest challenges and my biggest transformations came from what I learned and studied because of them.

I worked on a regulation-driven transformation project the organization had failed to implement for years. Some of the changes were drastic, effecting the core business, the technology, and basically everything in the company. Nobody welcomed the changes because they were regulatory and heavy. Several project managers worked successively on the change over the years, but they all left disappointed by the low priority given to the program and the difficulty delivering on the plan. Then the regulation authorities gave them a deadline.

The company was given a specific date by which they must comply with the regulations or be prohibited from doing business with its main customers or partners. The loss would be too much for the company to bear, which would have been a disaster costing them their lead in the market.

Nobody could even think of such a tragedy for the company, so the transformation was clearly urgent, and the project that had been pushed back year after year become the top priority. Budget? Didn't matter—only meeting the deadline mattered!

The challenges were numerous. Implementing new technology forced teams to learn on the job. Separating legacy systems that had been there for over twenty years was challenging. Documentation for many of those systems was nonexistent. A lot of guesswork was required, and collaborating with the few elders still in the company helped tremendously.

We experienced serious delays and cultural disagreements by outsourcing. We were in an economic crisis, where many external consultants were let go, and part of the solution was to fill their positions with a new development center in India. Technical infrastructure we ordered were seriously delayed. The changes included many legal issues with third parties, as well.

We took tremendous risk moving systems that the entire country's financial industry depended on. There was barely six hours to complete each server or system move or, in case of failure, to do a rollback.

The server move was strategically planned and had been prepared for months in advance but we only a six-hour window to validate the moves. The stress was significant, for there was much uncertainty with the most challenging cases where both the migration and the eventual rollback had blocking issues. As a team, we backed each other up and gave it beyond our best. I sometimes felt that whatever the disaster could be, we would pull through it, and we always did.

Since the program covered the company's core business, all departments were involved. We did not have one team but multiple teams working at the same time. Regardless of the tension we experienced at the start, we always ended up collaborating in the best ways. Some of the elders were most reluctant to help at first, but later, they were my biggest supporters as I led the program to completion.

I spent little time at my desk but was all over the buildings, working with others, coordinating, analyzing, and building teams. The people I worked with were very competent. I can say this about many of organizations I work with, even the ones where the implementation fails, but the difference here was the team spirit and the commitment to our shared mission. This was my most successful project of all time simply for how we could overcome challenges as a team.

Everything was challenging in all possible ways, but as dedicated people on a mission and with a shared vision, nothing could stop us from delivering the transformation. We achieved in one year what could not be achieved during the previous three years.

When you work with a competent, able, and willing team, any challenges you might face, you overcome. Better than that, people are transformed in the process, even if sometimes they may work so hard that they fall on their knees.

I remember once, a recruiter was interviewing me and was worried that I might not stay long with a client he wanted to send me to. I answered that I was loyal to my customers, and as a consultant, I would bring the best help to them, and when my work was done, I would be happy to leave for another client who needed me. I am committed to my profession as an IT management consultant and a change leader. I am not committed to a particular job or position. Each position is an opportunity for me to contribute to a client and to my own growth both as a person and a professional. I may need a paycheck, but my motivation is greater than that—it is my purpose, my divine assignment.

Being a consultant is not about sitting in a comfortable place and feeling secure. For me, it is about helping organizations and people solve challenging problems. I contribute to their organization success, and they contribute to my growth.

Then there is the unfortunate situation where a great, loyal worker leaves, the rest disengage, and the company becomes like a boat in a storm without a captain. It can happen to any company that does not approach change strategically or underestimates its effects. It happens to the best companies.

At one great company, I observed the following points that brought it to a tumultuous situation:

- lack of support from top management
- implementing change projects like normal projects
- lack of employee recognition
- no change support team
- poor communication

Performing in such a situation when one is exhausted or having personal/family/health issues is challenging. Your ability to stay afloat, swim, or, in some cases, drift along through the storm is inestimable.

SUMMARY

The best achievements and the worst failures have a common denominator: people's fears. People's endurance and experience and how they are supported will make the difference. The support team should be created with people who are prepared to lead and can handle people's fears, guide them, and help make their journey a transformative one.

Fears must be addressed correctly, and choosing leaders who are emotionally intelligent and able to work through the stress is a priority. Then the next step is supporting these people as they grow to be better leaders.

TAKING ACTIONS!

1. Find your organization's structure and identify the different units or departments that will need support.
2. Depending on the size of these units or departments, decide whether to allow one or more leaders onto the support group. It is often best to have two people per department acting as one principal leader and a backup.
3. Identify up to five people you consider leaders for these units. Did some of these people distinguish themselves after the change announcement? Find out who did it more strategically.
4. Rate each of these leaders on a scale of one to five on the criteria below (you may add more of your own). You may find this information from an official assessment in the company if there is one.
   a. trustworthiness
   b. teamwork
   c. ability to take risks
   d. authentic leadership
   e. communication
   f. involvement
   g. respect for others
   h. problem-solving abilities
   i. professional skills
   j. emotional skills

CHAPTER SEVEN

Innovation—How I Invented the Smartphone Before Steve Jobs

The only way you survive is you continuously transform into something else. IT's this idea of continuous transformation that makes you an innovation company.

— GINNY ROMETTY

It was 2001, and I was an MBA student at United Business Institutes (UBI) in Brussels. I had been living in Belgium for four years, and the previous three years, I had been fighting to keep my identity, my dreams, my innovative mindset, my aspiration, and my marriage alive.

I grew unhappy and my husband and I drifted apart. I knew I would not be able to handle a situation where others tried to control me and made me live somebody else's life. Soon, I decided to take back my freedom.

At that time, I was working for a well-known, international IT consulting company. One of the first things I did as I was claiming my destiny was to pursue my dream of earning an MBA. I already had a bachelor's in business management and two associates of applied science degrees, respectively, in technology and food science and technology. I choose to combine both my business management and technology educations. Two of my professional enterprises that I am most passionate about. I was admitted to UBI for my MBA specializing in managing information technology. The innovator in me who had been repressed was coming alive again.

I remember, the first month into my courses, I saw this young businesswoman, elegant, positive, professional, and smart. She was so talkative and witty once we introduced ourselves to each other. I was drawn to her, and we met and become teammates on our first group work assignment. Her name was Krisztina Pinter—an expat just like me, Krisztina was a marketing manager for Sony in Belgium. We got along very well, and as a marketer for a technology product, Krisztina did well selling many of Sony's new product lines to me. Our profiles were very complementary. She is a passionate marketer, and she met her match in me as a technology enthusiast and innovator. I end up purchasing several Sony products from computer to camera and many gadgets in between at great price, facilitated by Krisztina. I was always happy about my purchases, except for one device, the palm pilot.

As a technology professional, my passion for technology came only after my passion for business. I choose to learn information technology in 1995, because I saw that it would serve business and life in general. I am not a geek, but I have a more practical approach to technology, which is, "show me how you can make or contribute to making life (personal and professional) better." When I got that, I was well into a food science and technology degree, but I did not want to do life without information technology, so I went for a double major, overcoming all the associated obstacles. Technology has been a way to make the impossible dream possible.

After a couple of weeks using the palm pilot, I was frustrated and disappointed. I have always written notes, goals, and questions in journals or fancy little notebooks since I was a child. With the palm pilot, I was excited that I would be able to enhance my habits. But two weeks after I got it, I was telling Krisztina how the palm pilot is the dumbest innovation I've seen and how much potential I saw in the idea of such a little gadget.

I explained to Krisztina about the tremendous potential I saw with such a tool being connected with other devices so I could access the internet, things in my home, people in my network, and other functions that would simplify my life. I explain how busy my life is working during the day and going to school in the evening, and that sometimes, I lack the time even for grocery shopping. My days were packed, and this palm pilot could help much better than it was helping. As a technologist, that was why I choose information technology, and this tool had let me down. Krisztina listened to my rants and told me that I was right, it could be better, but it was all she had for sale with Sony. I remember laughing and saying, "Of course, you are the marketing professional, and I am the information technology professional."

Then a few terms later, we were both taking an entrepreneurship class in the MBA program. Our professor, Dr. Olivier Hance, ask us to create teams and for each team to work on a project for the course. I asked Krisztina if she remembered the palm pilot and did she want to turn it into a technology success story with me. She said yes, and I was thrilled.

By then, ideas were coming into my mind hundreds per minute, and I remember having to wake up in the middle of the night to write down functionality ideas for the new, smarter version of the palm pilot. Krisztina, as a technology lover, was enthusiastic and had even more insight into the possibilities and features we talked about. We ended up splitting the work at some point, with frequent meetings to align. She was brilliant with the financial plan and the marketing plan. I was entirely absorbed by both the technology and software innovations and all possibilities it would offer to all types of people. All of which Krisztina captured very well and translated into the marketing plan. *She surely knows how to sell this thing*, I thought. I could not have asked for a better teammate.

Then came our final presentation for the entrepreneurship class and the submission of our business plan. Both Krisztina and I were on fire. The project had drawn out what was best in each of us. Dr. Hance was very impressed with both the details in our project and our enthusiasm as we delivered our speech. He had invited the MBA students and a panel of professionals to his home for the final entrepreneurship project. Krisztina and I got praise and an A+ for our project, which was identical to today's smartphone.

After we graduated from our MBA program, I asked Krisztina to consider turning our project into a business venture. Unfortunately, neither of us had the financial capacity and dedication to raising capital for such a project. Krisztina saw no point taking the risk with her career, as she was doing well at Sony and wanted to continue there only. On my side, soon after, I would suffer from the global stock market crash and job loss. This new reality was so different and starting from zero, with no funds, was difficult.

Fortunately, I have this gift where I don't just see what is but what can be. It has been a blessing, as well as a challenge. Many times, I had to restrain myself to fit in. I choose a consultancy career, as it is the type of work that best aligns with who I am. I am a delivery-focused problem solver, a leader in challenging situations. I can quickly grasp a situation, propose solutions, and implement them. When I am done delivering, I am pushed to find the next mission, regardless of job security. My mission is stronger than my need for a job, and it is true that the day you find your mission, you never have a job anymore. but you just keep working on your mission, regardless of the jobs you have to do to achieve your purpose.

I always knew my purpose and my mission. But last month, while taking an executive education program with a specialization in innovation and strategy, with Dr. Phil Budden and Professor Hal Gregersen, the authors of *The Innovator's DNA,* my personality and dominant traits were identified—My Innovator DNA. I am a delivery-focused Innovator. I felt, "I am with the right company." I thought for the first time that I was somewhere I didn't have to justify myself, my choices, drive, mission, and purpose.

Conceiving, managing, and delivering innovative technology projects drives me. I have experienced plenty of this in the last twenty years in Europe and America, and with the Global changes that took place in every sector. However, innovation does not belong to a particular type of person only. Everyone is capable of innovation, though some people are more natural innovators. It's easier if you have some natural tendencies toward innovation, but anyone can learn how to innovate and practice innovating.

For organizational innovation, the best results are generated using innovation as a process within existing business processes. For the innovation process, the more participants contributing to a managed approach, the better the results.

Innovation can be created by:

- Improving an existing product or solution.
- Providing a solution for an existing problem.
- Creating solutions/products that did not exist or are in demand.
- Optimizing the efficiency or appreciation of an existing product or service by creating supporting products or services around the main one.

In all cases, innovation can be supported by questioning and brainstorming.

It is also important to define the innovator DNA of your project leaders so you can create a harmonious team with complementary leaders.

If you wish to know your innovator's DNA and how to develop innovation in your organization, I invite you to join my Executive Innovators group. There you can take the innovator DNA test and learn more about your natural abilities. You can also learn how to structure your leadership team to get the best digital transformation leadership team and how to drive innovation in your organization.

SUMMARY

Innovators are people who question the status quo. You've heard the old saying, "If it is not broken, don't fix it." This is not in line with an innovator's mentality, as the innovator sees beyond what is. The innovator sees what can be. The innovator does not have to have all the ideas. They can work with other people's ideas, points of view, and needs. That is why, in your organization, you should consider everyone a contributor to innovation. Whatever their specialty or business unit, anyone with a crazy idea may be able to sow the seeds of a significant, breakthrough transformation. The requirement is that innovation must be part of the business process and be managed.

TAKING ACTIONS

- Identify essential products or critical processes that, if improved, would most benefit the organization.
- Create a manageable innovation group consisting of people involved in the product or process and also some people who are not.
- Do an innovation session where you ask the people on the team to question the product or process. Limit this session to asking questions that could lead to identifying possible improvements. Do not put forth possible answers at this time.

- Do another brainstorming session where you ask the group to think about ways the product/service could be improved.
- Review the suggestions, capturing those with the most potential for improving the product or process.
- Make this a recurring activity, and use it to highlight innovative ideas related to all aspects of your organization.

Note: You can also do this with customers when working on improving the customer experience.

CHAPTER EIGHT

Planning Strategically End-To-End

In preparing for battle, I have always found that plans are useless, but planning is indispensable.
— *Dwight D. Eisenhower*

Eisenhower's quote reinforces the need for strategic planning. We don't do strategic planning for the plan itself but to understand the situation we have at hand. The plan will change constantly, but because we strategize, we are less likely to be taken by surprise or give up. That is because in strategic planning, we plan for the worst and then take calculated risks and prepare contingencies to address the risks. The plan is an output, not the goal, which is to be strategically prepared.

With that in mind, let's strategize change implementation for your organization's transformation.

STRATEGIC PLANNING EQUALS PREPARATION

What is a plan but one of multiple outputs? A plan is a map to help us reach our destination. It is a tool that helps us monitor and control. If one exit or a road is closed or blocked, knowing the environment allows us to find a detour, another road, or an overlooked way to our destination.

Sometimes with your plan, when every way is blocked or when you are constantly banging against walls, knowing your environment will allow you to create a way out. That's the power strategic planning gives you.

Too often, we use the plan as a sacred or perfect tool. It is not! Worrying too much about following the plan or being upset when the plan changes indicates poor strategic planning.

Transformation is made of multiple change projects. In a change or transformation project, our plan will change more often than with a standard or routine project. The only way around that is smart strategic planning. In planning strategically, we should identify the different phases of a transformation project and, for each phase, the multiple factors where additional changes may occur and seriously impede the project. Then consider contingencies for each.

But wait—for a change project, besides the known changes, the most challenging aspects are the "unknown changes or the further impacted areas." These unknown changes are the multiple way in which the initial or planned change affects the organization's environment (businesses, units, projects, technology, etc.). Changes have consequences, and these consequences have a ripple effect, causing changes in other areas, leading to further changes in dependencies and so on. Said otherwise, most changes affect many different parts of the business. Then these changes bring further changes on additional aspects of the business. For each change made to a given system, the downstream effects must be identified not only on directly dependent systems but also on other systems that depend on the system being changed.

GET TOP MANAGEMENT ONBOARD OR PREPARE TO BURN OUT

While I expect that your digital transformation was initiated and supported by, and is a priority for top management, I must acknowledge from experience that sometimes this support is undermined by changes in the organization's goals or situation.

More and more, businesses and projects go beyond in-house teams, where the organization owns each resource. We now work more with matrix organizations, with centers of expertise and/or business units delivering "services." Key organizations may be local, national, international, or global. Your strategic planning scope needs to extend as wide as your organization does.

Let's take KOB, a digital transformation program within an organization named Kalix.

The KOB program will change the way clients access information, pay their bills, and get support. To make this happen, the digital transformation leader works with different business units and services within the organization, collaborating with:

- multiple product/service managers to gather specific information about their products to base the billing on;
- multiple application owners/analysts for information on the applications that support these products/services;
- customer service department(s) to prepare to support the changes once implemented;
- technical teams responsible for the servers, network, telecommunications, and security;
- teams that test the different applications;
- data teams analyzing and managing the databases;
- development leaders;
- process-improvement department;
- billing department;
- sales department;
- marketing department; and
- purchasing department.

Sometimes you can't tell which aspects of the organization will be affected until further analysis is done. At times, it can be difficult to include all the leaders even when your change may affect them all. Your best bet is to have the person accountable to all, such as the CEO or CIO (local or global, according to the scope) involved, even if they intervene only with major events or at some steering-committee meetings.

While the person most involved in change implementation among top management is the CIO, when it comes to digital transformation, all C-suite executives are import to your success. Involving the CEO, the CIO, and the CFO is mandatory—the CEO for all business and organization decisions, the CIO for all information technology decisions, and the CFO for all financial investments. Depending on the organization's size, the above leaders may delegate some of their responsibilities to one or more other executives.

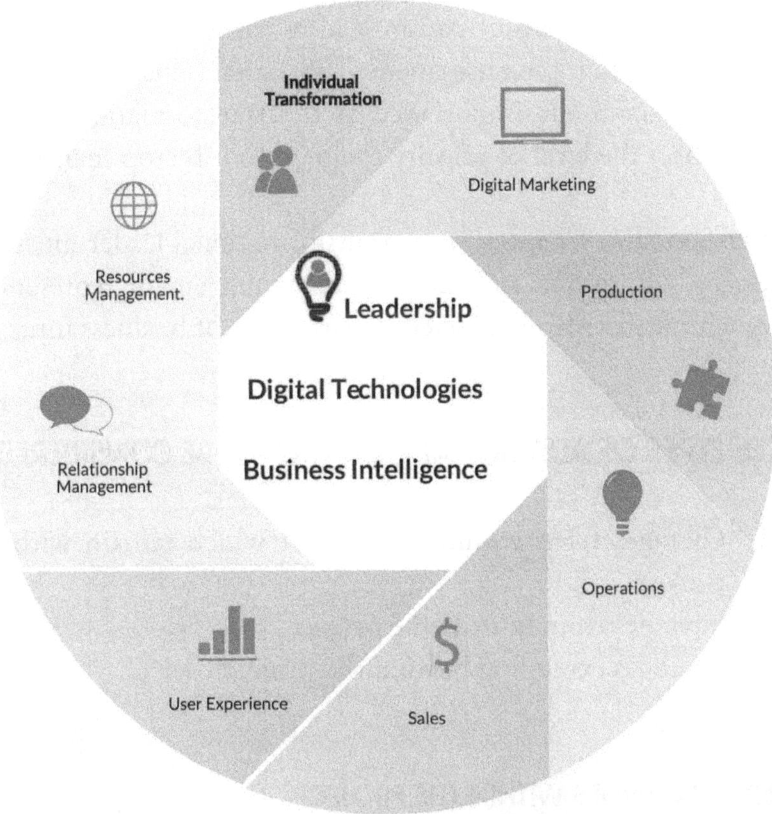

The Digital Transformation Roadmap

When change effects multiple business units, departments, and projects, everyone involved is motivated by their own responsibilities and interests. The CEO has a global interest in the organization as a whole.

Digital transformation requires investment in multiple resources, such as technology, machinery, and human resources. The CFO will be needed to align such investments and establish their estimated return on investment with the CEO and CIO.

Therefore, digital transformation leaders cannot do their job without support from top management. The digital transformation leader must understand the importance of the transformation project or program and the level of priority assigned to it by top management.

As mentioned in Chapter 2, the transformational leader must create a steering committee and include top management representation along with leaders from affected departments or business units.

THREE TYPES OF ADDITIONAL CHANGES TO BE CONSIDERED

1. Changes from within the project which remain within the project
2. Changes from outside the project
3. Changes extending beyond the project

POINT 1: CHANGES WITHIN THE PROJECT THAT REMAIN WITHIN THE PROJECT

Change leaders have more control over changes within the digital transformation project than outside changes. Contingencies in repose to these changes are researched and considered.

Murphy's Law—whatever can go wrong will go wrong—is actually a good way to look at strategic planning when it comes to possible internal changes that may result from a change project. Also remember that whatever can go wrong is likely to do so at the worst possible moment. This is not pessimism but preparation—prepare for the worst while working for the best outcome.

Strategize this way!

1. Identify the key deliverables of each phase.
2. Identify what could stop or delay that key deliverable.
3. Identify, on a scale of one to five, how likely it is that this risk will occur.
4. Identify what you and your team can do to reduce the risk.
5. Identify what you will do if it (or something similar) happens despite your efforts.

POINT 2: CHANGES FROM OUTSIDE THE PROJECT IDENTIFY DEPENDENCIES BETWEEN BUSINESSES, PROCESSES, OR PROJECTS

The most challenging issues come from either being dependent on outside organizations or extending transformation projects beyond your organization. Such issues are the bottlenecks that cause delays, failure, and conflicts, leading to wasted time, energy, and investments.

EXAMPLES OF EXTENDED CHANGES:

- change in shared procedures across multiple projects
- change in a technology/tool/system shared by several projects, departments, or businesses
- change in a shared team within and outside of the project
- changes in a shared execution schedule

- change in a shared database
- change in one or more services used to support the solution or product delivery
- change in a tool or solution owned by an external provider

The truth with extended change is that you may never know how far reaching the changes may be and how vital quick decisions and actions are to sorting out the situation.

These extended changes are the reason involving top management in the change project/program from the start is essential. The project leader or change leader's authority is often limited to the project's scope.

Ripple-effect changes on the business, department, or project emanating from the transformation may be identified from the start, though it is not always possible. Sometimes, businesses, projects, and/or units are affected in ways we could not foresee. If top management was not involved, alignment or collaboration can be challenging. That is especially true if a given area has nothing to gain directly from the change.

POINT 3: CHANGES EXTENDING BEYOND THE PROJECT

This applies especially for the solution supplier or when the solution is used by one or more external parties or clients.

Besides top management, involving client representatives or third party provider is necessary for business alignment and reducing risk.

The power of communication, risk analysis (business and technical), and decision-making is important in this case. Change leaders absolutely must rely on top-management support for aligning the parties involved.

Consider the following 2Cs (two change types) formula for better change preparation and planning.

THE 2CS SOLUTION FOR THE CHANGE'S ORIGIN:

- internal change: contingencies
- external or extended impacts change: contingencies and collaborative alignment

IDENTIFYING DEPENDENCIES AND AFFECTED AREAS

The best way to approach the impact analysis is with a simple graphic flow chart that provides a helicopter view for identifying the affected areas.

Start the flow chart with:

1. business and organization's overview;
2. main change area(s);
3. other areas connected to or dependent upon those change area(s);
4. systems within the other areas and how they are linked;
5. system components that will be changed;
6. sub-components, modules, and tools that will be changed;
7. deliverables (operations, projects, and business) effected in various areas; and
8. the affected stakeholders.

IMPACT LEVEL, SEVERITY, AND TIMING

Not all consequences carry the same weight. A change leader should not only know about their project/business but must also understand the overall structure of the organization and how various departments are linked. For example, review impact severity as follows:

A. high impact, low consequence
B. high impact, high consequence
C. low impact, high consequence
D. low impact, low consequence

Some of these qualifications may apply to other operations, projects, or business units at different times.

For example, a change affecting the billing department may be qualified as, A: high impact and low consequences on the second week of the month, because the team has time to react before the critical billing period at the end of the month. However, late in the month, that same change would be qualified as, B: high impact, high consequence for the billing department.

The same change, starting on a different date, may be classified as, C: low impact, low consequence, because the billing department has sufficient time to implement the new system.

Therefore, it is important for a change-project manager to explore the organization. Knowledge of the dependent or linked systems is critical to the project or program. It is important to know the key operation dates, such as the dates of events and future plans. Also consider major risks, contingencies, and key leaders. This is essential for proper risk management and strategic planning. Although not required, this is what makes the difference between leaders who get results and those who don't.

Knowing that, you understand that tasks in your planning change, and you are not taken aback. Instead, you understand that nothing is fixed, and what makes the difference is how prepared you are and how well you know the organization, the people, and environment that you are working in.

This information will help you tremendously in leading effectively and resolving conflicts, problem solving, and managing risks. When conflicting interests arise, you will be able to present enough facts and relevant information to the steering committee and CIO to help them make an informed decision.

Your plan will change, and though having a plan is important for staying on course, mastering strategic planning that allows you to adjust when needed is even more important. It is the knowledge and insight you need to lead and deal with situations that may arise.

Unfortunately, many organizations lose time, money, and energy dealing with conflicts of interest between units due to lack of information, selfishness, and poor collaboration. Always work *with* your colleagues in other units of the organization, not against them! When someone works against their colleagues from other departments, that person undermines the work of the CIO and the top management, and puts the organization and its investment at risk. Be a transformational leader for all stakeholders; show fair play.

As a transformational leader, your change project/program's scope goes beyond its official charter and expands to your organization's business goals. Once you understand that, you will be able to do strategic planning differently and embrace the role of transformational leader.

YOU MUST KNOW WHERE YOU ARE GOING TO GET THERE

It may sound silly to say this, but if you don't know what you expect to achieve or where you want to go with the changes you want to implement, you will never get there.

What is it you are trying to achieve? Is it the full vision? Is it part of the vision? Strategically planning your digital transformation implementation indicates that you have an end-to-end plan with a clear view of what you want to achieve. It implies that you know the deliverables at each phase.

I have seen large organizations with multiple teams working on different components of a product but with each team working in their corner or even secretly on the side. When the time comes to integrate the components, the teams find out that the components do not fit together. This often starts a blame war. But it is simply a failure in strategic planning facilitated by an environment that encourages teams to work against each other instead of together.

CREATING YOUR FOOLPROOF END-TO-END STRATEGIC PLAN

Even if not well detailed yet, you must create your strategic plan and include:

- roadmaps
- phases

- milestones
- entry criteria
- exit criteria
- control points
- prerequisites
- estimates
- final delivery
- post-delivery or closure activities

Regardless of task breakdowns and the teams involved in a transformation project, always have clear expectations of all involved. Team members must know what they should deliver, to whom, when, and with specific quality criteria. You and your team should be able to analyze and prepare for final delivery based on the milestones along the way. The components may change over time, but it is important to identify them, update them, and inform the team.

End-to-end strategic planning is necessary for monitoring and course correction and for a successful end-to-end change implementation. Don't get lost in the details, and make sure you have a full strategy in sight, even when you don't know how to fill in the details yet. The leadership team will help you fill in those missing details later. For now, have your full official end-to-end plan and scope in sight. That way, you will be better prepared for your extended scope.

SPECIAL CONSIDERATIONS

Give special considerations to the following factors for your digital transformation project, for they are factors likely to become extended or broadened.

1. Type of organization and culture
2. Business and IT alignment
3. Reinforced risk management
4. International team involvement
5. Security and disaster-recovery planning
6. Data size and scope

ORGANIZATIONAL CHOICES AND CULTURE

Transformation overcomes and bridges distances within the team and organization. Regardless of differences in culture, countries, time zones, or competencies, implementing changes requires teams to work together.

Whether you are working locally, internationally, with a global team, or as a transformational leader, your goal is to get the team to work together harmoniously to deliver the vision. Team and organizational aspects must be part of your strategic planning. The challenges of a global team spread over several continents, in different time zones, with different languages and cultures are different than that of a local team in the same building, speaking the same language (though this does not guarantee understanding).

Strategic planning allows you, as a transformational leader, to identify the challenges, the risks, and bridge the gap by providing solutions that help minimize those challenges and risks.

THE ORGANIZATION MODEL

I've seen that with most change implementation, we go from the hierarchical organization model to a matrix, because it allows for a better use of resources. The big issue that causes many failures in change management is creating a matrix environment (often incomplete) and just throwing people into it without aligning them based on skills, interests, and experience. Then individuals fall into a matrix organization's pitfalls of responsibility and accountability in areas they are not familiar with.

FROM THE TRIANGLE TO THE RECTANGLE: PEOPLE EXPERIENCE

While the traditional project management model uses the triangle to illustrate how to manage time, cost, and scope, change projects require more than that. They require managing people's experiences during uncertainty. Therefore, my model for change management or transformational leadership is a rectangle, which includes leading people as one of the main pillars.

The Traditional Project Management Triangle

The Project Management Triangle

The traditional project management schema here fosus on managing time, cost and scope.

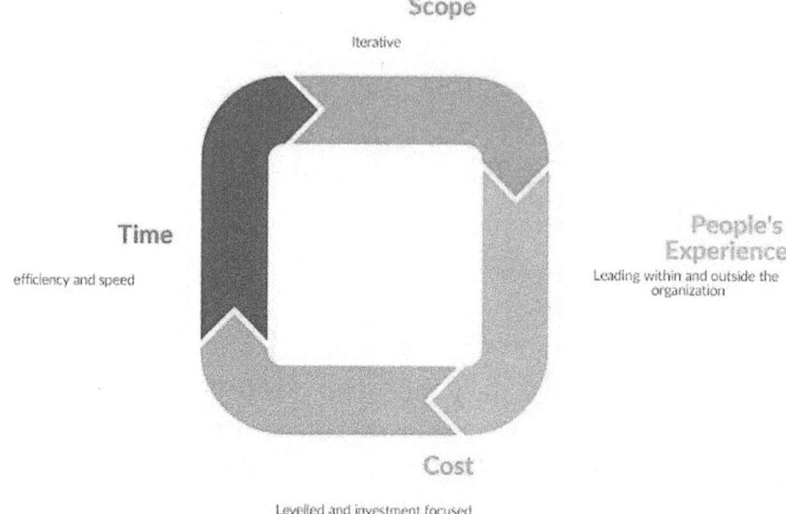

We must understand that people's experiences alone can determine success or failure, not only for the project, but also for the organization or business' future success.

A transformational leadership team extends beyond the official team to the organization's people (sometimes external people, as well). Collaborating with other team leaders outside of the change project is essential to making change happen. To collaborate effectively with other leaders, you must know about their business, their priorities, their key dates, and what matters to them. Knowing how your change project may affect others' interests and vice versa is the basis of collaborating to reach the best outcome for the organization.

The transformational leader who does not show concern and respect for others' operations and interests breaks the collaborative spirit necessary to achieve a transformed organization. This starts even more business conflict, leading to personal conflicts.

Unit leaders may bring information, facts, and options to the digital transformation leader so the leader can make strategic decisions for IT as a business. However, bringing personal conflicts, anger, and accusations to an executive to judge indicates a lack of professionalism and a poor use of the executive's time.

Leaders who can work out their conflicts, overcome negative emotions, take responsibility, support each other, and facilitate business flow are what organizations need and search for today. There is less and less time to waste in destructive conflicts that bring down people and the organization. Also, time to market is becoming shorter and shorter for the technology business, so who can afford to waste time?

I have seen many respected organizations lose some of their key players because of poor change implementation causing many to jump ship. I have also seen these key players working for competitors—all because of a poor experience and loss of hope or confidence in a company that they once loved.

ALIGNING BUSINESS AND IT

We've all heard or maybe experienced the blame-games between business and IT departments. Having worked on both sides, I am rather familiar with the arguments.

Here are the most used arguments. Operations says, "It is IT's fault that it's too complicated and can't be delivered on time."

IT says, "It is operations' fault they did not provide clear specifications or that they required too many changes, sometimes at the last minute."

Transformation eases the work both for IT and operations. No more distant conversations and hiding progress or delayed decisions. The two must work together on a regular basis. IT and the rest of the organization must deliver teamwork, regardless of which team each may belong to. We are a team delivering together, regardless of accountability and responsibility. Having the business analyst work closely with the IT team, regardless of location, becomes mandatory due to the speed of change.

Changes and their effects are so widespread and happen so quickly that whatever impact analysis is being carried out, it should be both business and technical. It must take into account other ongoing changes.

REINFORCING RISK MANAGEMENT

This is where knowing the organization pays off. When the organization's units are identified and their business and systems are understood, risks and contingencies can be analyzed.

Business and system dependencies help identify risks and elaborate on contingencies wherever applicable.

GLOBAL TEAM CONSIDERATIONS

With global and international teams, more risks stemming from communication challenges, time differences, cultural misunderstandings, work approaches, and such are to be considered. While we create contingency plans for risk, strategies or facilities must be put in place for a global team—for example, team-building exercises, improved communication courses, time alignments, diversity workshops, and so forth should be put in place and be part of end-to-end planning as a way to improve team effectiveness and performance. The goal is to create or make up for the advantages that proximity allows in building teams and relationships. This is a way to improve productivity and is a must for global and international teams.

PLANNING FOR SECURITY AND DISASTER RECOVERY

This is one big, sensitive subject. Disaster recovery was simpler years ago. Now, due to the need for improved security, disaster recovery planning (DRP) must take into account the security plan and procedures already in place. DRP is essential during change because disasters can come from outside (which is what we plan for most) or from inside as we proceed with the change. Disaster-recovery planning must take that into account as well.

DATA SCOPE AND SIZE

In identifying your full scope, you'll analyze and prepare appropriately but give double attention to the points above, as that's where the biggest challenges in change management arise.

Strategic planning is not a one-and-done job, but a continuous set of activities. It is continuously learning about and supporting your organization, and it is visioning and strategizing on how to best reach your goal through thick and thin. Having the helicopter view prepares you to strategize on and course correct multiple areas without losing sight of your vision. As a transformational leader, whether you are a CIO, a change leader, a director, or a project manager, strategize always, and always have more than one strategy for reaching your vision! Your team counts on you to lead them from start to finish. They don't want to arrive somewhere in the middle and hear you ask, "Now what?" Create your strategy end to end, even if there are holes in it.

SUMMARY

Strategic planning allows us to anticipate challenges, prepare for them, decrease risk, and create a positive experience while reaching our goals. Every plan is subject to changes, and that is normal because we live in an imperfect world. We do not do strategic planning for the plan itself but to be prepared. So, focus less on having a plan and more on exploring and analyzing possibilities. The more experienced you are, the more things you can prepare, so include your leadership team in the planning process to get the most from it. Strategic planning is essential for reaching business goals, so invest time and care into it.

TAKING ACTIONS!

1. Layout your complete scope for an end-to-end strategy.
2. Draft the flow and milestones (short and long term).
3. Identify the stakeholders.
4. Identify the risks and contingencies.
5. Link external risks to external stakeholders, systems, and so on.
6. Review your organization or reinvent it to facilitate quick decision-making and solution implementation.

7. Strategize how you will facilitate the change implementation, be it with a global team, support people, organization types, and all other subjects that matter to your organization.
8. Create your strategic plan so it includes not just a deliverables plan but also a facilitation plan.
9. Strategize about your disaster-recovery plan and security.
10. Include roles and responsibility in your plan (without naming anyone).

CHAPTER NINE

Digital Transformation Strategy vs. Business Strategy

The essence of strategy is choosing what not to do.
— Michael Porter

While digital transformation is powered by technology-centered innovation, the business must be in the driver's seat in order to take best advantage of it. Businesses that approach digital transformation as a technology opportunity neglect the benefits and the transformative powers of digital transformation. This chapter will show you how to create that digital transformation strategy from a business-leadership point of view, powered by innovative technology that is accepted and financed by the CFO and conceived of and led by a hybrid leader.

WHY EACH BUSINESS MUST CREATE ITS OWN DIGITAL STRATEGY

Every successful business is unique and has its own value proposition for its customers. The digital transformation strategy of each business should be a reflection of its objectives.

Let's review the digital technologies and the opportunities that they offer us.

1. ***Social Media.*** Online real-time communications and socialization has transformed how we connect with people and organizations and how we communicate and socialize globally.
2. ***Mobility.*** Almost everyone has a smartphone, and we take this little device everywhere with us. More than a phone, it is now a supercomputer that has already partly or completely replaced watches, bedside clocks, daily calendars, computers, offices, libraries, and cameras. More than that, it has become our radio and TV, giving us access to the world. Our mobile phone connects to the internet so that we can access anything online wherever we are and move our world with us. Some additional technological functions include a scanner, GPS, a sensor, a camera, a live broadcasting station, a payment wallet, a signature device, and an access badge. That's true mobility.
3. ***Internet of Things (IoT).*** The interconnection of things in real time over the internet, wherever their location may be, and the exchange of information about their interaction are known as the Internet of Things or IoT. This allows us to control, track, and monitor anything at any distance, anywhere. With that, we can automate systems plus receive precious information and analysis. Coupled with social media, the Internet of Things allows us to share that information in real

time over the web. Sharing over the internet, especially when done emotionally, allows us to reach more people and create viral effects. This alone has transformed marketing drastically. Therefore, IoT and social media give us control over things and situations anytime and anywhere through a network and the power to influence people and the world in real time.

4. ***Artificial Intelligence (AI).*** Artificial intelligence is a true game changer as it is an intelligence that supports human intelligence with its multiple disciplines, such as machine learning, robotics, deep learning, neural networking, natural language processing (NLP), which offer unprecedented opportunities to transform business and organizations with automation assistance and performing tasks that are more challenging for humans but easy for machines. While there are worries about artificial intelligence replacing human intelligence, this is not a reality. Artificial intelligence is supporting human intelligence but cannot completely replace human intelligence. As a MIT Sloan certified AI strategist, I help businesses and organizations adopt the new business intelligence, which is the correct combination of AI and human intelligence for each business. Powered by big data or data science and the correct strategy, AI is the one main technology that will bring the most innovation to our world.
5. ***Big Data and Data Science.*** The term Big Data refers to the volume of all the information that we create, monitor (online and offline), process, save, and share. It includes text, metrics, videos, photos, graphics, audio, and documents. Data Science is the science that is helping us uncover all the possibilities and methods for leveraging data. This infinite amount of data is captured by all means online and offline using the Internet of Things, the internet, intranets, and governmental systems, together becoming Big Data. Such a large amount of data

demands greater storage and processing capacity than that of our home computers and organizations' servers to make efficient use of the asset. Therefore, the need for fast processing and storage of that infinite data leads to the next digital-technology pillar, Cloud Computing.

6. ***Cloud Computing.*** This technology allows us to store all of this information, exchange it, multiply it, access it, and process it rapidly. Cloud computing has literally cleared our offices and our homes from computers, servers, mainframes, and large server rooms and changed the technology industry forever. Furthermore, it makes data storage, data processing, and business intelligence accessible and affordable to smaller businesses.
7. ***Blockchain and Bitcoin.*** Blockchain technologies and bitcoin are extreme decentralization technologies and, respectively, a secured, global, accurate, and decentralized ledger with no single owner and, a peer to peer electronic, decentralized cash system. We are in the infancy of the disruptive possibilities that blockchain and bitcoin technologies can and will offer.

Within the technology evolution lies the true opportunity for businesses and organizations to transform and reinvent themselves, making them more agile, closer to consumers, more scalable, efficient, and thus more successful. This is called digital transformation. However, beyond technology, it takes true leadership to create the proper vision for each business or organization and to implement that vision successfully so that it leads to the business' digital transformation.

Digital technologies combined with business practices, leadership skills, and creativity allow leaders to transform businesses, organizations, and the world in ways beyond our imaginations. Your vision is limitless and so is your creativity. The question is, what do you want to achieve with your business, your organization, and/or your team? You have the transformative vision. Now, how can you put all these precious resources together to achieve that vision? That's what we are going to explore now.

BRIDGING THE GAP BETWEEN BUSINESS AND IT

For technology to best support business, IT leaders must know and understand the objectives and interests of the business and then align to them. It could appear simple, but the reality shows that it is not. Furthermore, business and IT people are not always aligned with the same understanding of the functions of the business. Many costly project failures have their root cause in misunderstandings between business and IT, either from the start or at some point during the IT development life cycle.

Leading digital transformation, therefore, is about business transformation inspired by technology and achieved by transformed leaders and organizations. In no case should IT be leading the business, or we will fall into the digital-fashionista trap. Digital-fashionista is a term I use to refer to organizations that use digital technologies just like how garments are used in the fashion industry. They use the digital technologies that are in style and change for the next trend; even though the technology may not help them reach their goals, they still want the latest ones. The issue is that often, they don't have a digital strategy or at least not an in-depth one with sustainable goals. They may spend a fortune on the next best technology, but without a proper digital transformation strategy, they will continue to experience the same disillusion because the approach is based on a fake hope. If they don't change their approach to focus on strategy first, they are highly likely to fail in the next few years.

If there is too much focus on the technology, you are then developing costly technical solutions that no one really needs or wants. If there is too much focus on the business, you may neglect the tools that amplify and optimize your solutions. If there is not enough focus on the people implementing the solution, you could get an organization with disengaged resources, conflicts, and business/organizational chaos.

Your digital transformation strategy should envelope the strategies that will help in creating the business vision.

1. Business Intelligence Strategies
   a. What do your customers and prospects want?
   b. What experience do you want to give to your customers now and in the future?
   c. What do you know about customer preference, lifestyle, wishes, and personal or professional evolution?
   d. How are you creating and delivering solutions to your market(s) today and in the future?
   e. Are you making data speak loud enough by analyzing it?
   f. How profitable are the above strategies for your business?
   g. What are the latest innovations in the industry/business?
2. Technology Strategies
   a. What technologies and systems does your organization invest in? Are these technologies making the business more efficient and productive, and how is it measured?
   b. How do you make sure that the technology is well chosen, correctly implemented, used, adopted, and supported?
3. Organization and People Strategies
   a. How do you help your organization grow and transform while innovating continuously?
   b. How do you help individuals grow and progress within the organization while investing in them?

Let's take the example of Amazon, a company I love because it gives me such a great customer experience. I may not cover all of Amazon's business strategies, but there are many inspiring ones here.

BUSINESS-INTELLIGENCE STRATEGY

USER EXPERIENCE

Amazon allows a user, from the comfort of their home, to find books, sample them, order them, and have them delivered in one of two ways:

- physically, in a few days, or
- electronically, immediately using the Kindle, their own electronic reader, or in audio format via their "Audible format," and even in MP3.

Their multiformat delivery is a direct reflection of their digital-business model conceived to deliver to clients anytime, anywhere, by any means possible, and at different pricing levels, as long as the client wants it.

PRODUCT CREATION

Amazon determines what their customers' needs are and works backward to deliver it to them innovatively. Their Kindle tablet or electronic reader was their customers' wish rather than their engineer's dreams. If customers don't want something, it will not be pursued.

CUSTOMER SERVICE

At Amazon, customer service is everyone's job and not just customer service agents. They make it part of the user experience. Amazon approaches the user experience such that everyone in the company should be responsible for it. Complaints can be devastating to the whole company, especially in the age of viral tweets and blogs. Amazon CEO Jeff Bezos asks thousands of Amazon managers, including himself, to attend two days of call-center training each year. The payoff is humility and empathy for the customer.

Early on, Bezos brought an empty chair into meetings so "lieutenants" would be forced to think about the crucial participant who wasn't in the room—the customer. The customer's role is played by specially trained employees, dubbed "Customer Experience Bar Raisers." That way, customer service is integrated into the whole business flow.

DIGITAL MARKETING

Unlike the formal way of marketing to clients, Amazon believes that old-fashioned word of mouth has become even more important in the digital age. Therefore, preference is given to low-key process improvements that are meant to get happy customers buzzing.

DATA STRATEGY

Data science and business intelligence are to business what the brain is to the body.

Data is king at Amazon, particularly head-to-head tests of customer reactions to different features or site designs. Jeff Bezos, CEO of Amazon, calls it "a culture of metrics." Strategic information of interests and purchase history are captured, stored, analyzed, and used for innovation and future business development.

PRODUCTION AND PROCESSES

Amazon taps into digital technology to deliver everything that the customer wants while giving them multiple options at a reduced cost. Since Amazon's objectives are to dominate the information market, they get closer to their clients and maintain their domination objective with the following strategies.

a. Amazon cocreates with its suppliers (writers, authors, technology companies, delivery businesses, etc.) globally and invests in a global logistics system to get it done.
b. Amazon uses personal data smartly to know your interests and your purchase history and suggests new products accordingly. They use this information both to create delivery solutions and to sell them.
c. They suggest products to you according to what other people with interests similar to yours are reading.
d. Amazon even taps into the second-hand book market, which they know their clients somehow contribute to. They know that you may want to free space from your library and resell some of your purchases for second-hand profit. They create a parallel business of it and craft it so that it does not take away their existing market for new books. They remind you of that precisely.
e. Amazon knows that electronic storage is a big need for small and large businesses. Not only has it been profitable for them,

but in order to continue to dominate, they invest in becoming a cloud storage provider, therefore increasing their market share.

f. With their excellent technology and logistics systems, they know that they can deliver nearly anything, so they tap into businesses around the world, sharing with them and allowing them to sell their products online and use Amazon logistical systems and Amazon online stores that are created in a matter of minutes at no cost. That way, they have a whole new business model rather than that of a traditional (online) library.
g. Other types of information that Amazon taps into are graphics, pictures, and the film industry. Amazon invests in many more ventures that we hardly hear about to maintain their dominant position.
h. Amazon understands that information and business intelligence are behind every industry and every business. They break the rules of "specialization" and position themselves more as a digital-information and business-intelligence giant than as an online bookstore.

In addition to books, Amazon extends their business strategy to dominate digital-information delivery on multiple formats. Then they extend their business model by sharing their logistical systems and technology platforms. That way, they not only serve customers directly but also create several merchant partnerships at different levels.

Basically, whatever infrastructure or system they invest in for their business can be used as well to serve other businesses and further dominate the market.

The Amazon big-business strategy is not about the things they sell, as they understand that market needs change constantly. Their strategy will always be about delivering something that is more affordable in some way to their customers.

Their value proposition is made of three big constants:

1. Many options (formats)
2. Lower prices
3. Fast and reliable delivery

To facilitate this, they invest in their digital infrastructure and ventures with that main business-value proposition in mind.

TECHNOLOGY INVESTMENT STRATEGY

The Amazon technology-investment strategy follows its business strategy closely; therefore, investing in what they perceive as stability and preserving their business-value proposition of lower prices, multiple formats or selection, and fast and reliable delivery.

They also developed a new business model where they extend their market through sharing that technology and getting more return on their investment. This is done through:

- *Cloud technology, AI, Data-science and mobility*. They invest in their own need for storage as a core value of their business. Since their technology platform allows them to store so much data, why not share their storage power with other online businesses that have the same need? Thus, we have Amazon cloud storage for online businesses, facilitating businesses around the world.

- *Amazon Audible*. Amazon innovates and dominates their digital purchases through Audible, which delivers their value proposition faster.

The same digital technology approach for value proposition and business domination are also used in the following companies:

a. IMDB: movie delivery
b. Alexa.com: data science
c. DPReview: photography
d. Abebook: rare books
e. Twitch.tv: live streaming video

PEOPLE-INVESTMENT STRATEGY

Behind this innovative business, there is a global organization with a progressive mindset, prepared to make each delivery a success.

Beyond language, countries, culture, and political barriers, Amazon uses technology to break barriers and develop a global business model while dominating the market.

As said previously, everyone is trained to work in a call center for a few days. Amazon encourages innovation by trying, testing, and experiencing failures before succeeding. They encourage their people to be data driven and create new positions around that.

The company culture is well defined, and they invest in and push their people to continuously become more by innovating and achieving more. Data is king at Amazon, with what their CEO Jeff Bezos calls "a culture of metrics."

> *"Our culture is friendly and intense, but if push comes to shove, we'll settle for intense."*
>
> —*Jeff Bezos*

Digital Transformation Affects Every Sector and Every Industry

The Digital Transformation Success Formula
www.digitaltransformationleaders.com

SUMMARY

Great digital transformations are created from business vision and strategy. From your business vision, create the business strategy that will take advantage of digital technologies to allow your organization to achieve its goals. You can position your company as a disruptor in your industry, a market leader, or just a successful business. But if your business' transformative vision and strategy are nonexistent, no amount of digital technology can help your organization succeed. Use the following action-point questionnaire to create or improve your digital strategy. Be creative and step outside the box to innovate.

TAKING ACTIONS!

Here are a few questions to help you create or improve your business or organization's digital transformation strategy. They will help you brainstorm ideas for creating your digital strategy.

1. What business is the company in?
2. What are the big ideas or pillars of the business strategy that differentiate it from other businesses or organizations?
3. What is the business strategy that the IT system should support?
4. What are the main business units?
5. What are the business functions of each unit?
6. With what frequency are each of these functions used? Find out if each process or function is still relevant in the digital era.
7. Who does the business serve (specify each type of client)?
8. What is the projected (or existing) number of clients?
9. What are some key operations, their dates, and the frequencies for each business unit?
10. How does information flow between business units and business functions?
11. Who is responsible and accountable for each business unit?
12. Who is responsible and accountable for each business function?

13. What external links or inputs and outputs do we have within the business units?
14. How do we communicate across business units?
15. How do we communicate with consumers and at which phases?
16. What do we deliver to clients, when, and how?
17. What do we promise to clients in our marketing?
18. What customer service do we provide to clients and when?
19. How is IT compensated for its business and services for organizations that keeps IT as a service provider?
20. Who is accountable for IT compensation?
21. What are the business trends for today?
22. What are the expected or projected business trends for tomorrow?
23. What strategy do you have in place to gather relevant lifestyle information from consumers to analyze?
24. What could you cocreate with your consumers?
25. What could you cocreate with your suppliers?
26. How could you use digital technologies alone or in combination with business intelligence for any of the questions above to achieve any or all of the following?
    a. reduce costs
    b. reduce delays
    c. provide more options
    d. customize
    e. automate processing
    f. reduce prices
    g. get more relevant info from customers
    h. improve or deliver more services
    i. improve two-way communication
    j. improve delivery
    k. create more customer satisfaction

l. improve marketing efforts
m. improve sales
n. improve production

27. From which part of your facility can you develop another sustainable business model?

CHAPTER TEN

Digital Transformation Strategy vs. Technology Implementation

When you translate a dream into reality, it's never a full implementation. It is easier to dream than to do.

— Shai Agassi

Within the digital strategy is the technology strategy. Without the technology, there will not be digital transformation. And when it comes to technology, many choices are to be made, and these choices are crucial in the transformation's success. Chapter 10 shows how to approach the technology in a way that supports the business vision and goals in a sustainable way. It also addresses some common technology pitfalls to avoid and how to optimize technology implementation.

Developing a technology strategy follows the business strategy by facilitating, automating, and expanding it. Therefore, we will be building smart systems, automating them as much as possible, and making them reusable and reproducible.

LET THE BUSINESS DETERMINE THE PRIORITIES

The first step in developing information technology systems is to have clear business requirements that explain what the IT system should help the business achieve. The business function mapping and the priority order, along with business processes, must be clearly written with the help of a business analyst. The details of the business process and some approaches may be completed or reviewed later, but the business should know how they plan to create and deliver value to customers or ask IT to suggest specific ways to do so.

Because of that, the top management of the business needs relevant IT expertise, awareness, and knowledge of existing technology, technology innovation, feasibility, and what the organization can create. This knowledge in top management helps create better vision, expansion, and investment plans.

Now we are at the next step, which is about creating the business/IT system architecture with the collaborative help of business analysts, data scientists, and technology architects.

The IT system architecture should demonstrate how we go from point *A* to *Z* in the infrastructure and the main processing stops along the way.

The business-analysis document, when combined with the architecture document, should be clear in terms of business units, services, processes, data processing and storage capacity, technology stakeholders, and methods. For the stakeholders, at this stage, they should be seen as roles. Only after digital strategy is completed and project(s) have been executed should the roles be filled by the correct individuals.

Within IT organizations, there is a tendency to start developing systems and solutions before creating business document and system architecture. This is especially true when time is short and available resources are lacking. This is helpful to get ahead and prevent wasting time. However, for small projects the effects can be small, and for large projects and programs, such as digital transformation, they can get dramatic. It is essential to have at least a map of the technical architecture and business before going further in developing systems.

CHOOSING THE RIGHT TECHNOLOGY

The right technology for an organization is the one that will allow it to create its vision effectively, in less time, while delivering high quality results and providing the best return on the technology investment.

Digital transformation opens the door to a cheaper or more accessible technology solution. Part or all of the technology can be created, hosted, or rented for the technology strategy. It is all a matter of objectives, budget, competitiveness, and capacity.

DEVELOPING THE ORGANIZATION'S OWN TECHNOLOGY

It's better to create new technology that you can customize for your organization, versus using existing technology. This is the most expensive option but it is more flexible. It costs a company in development, maintenance, and upgrades. However, this approach, if well planned, may give the business a competitive edge, providing that the system performs well.

The rule would be that whatever you are developing, make it compliant with the market's standard protocols. Then integration and growth can take place easier, cheaper, and faster.

Development cycles are not as long as they used to be. It is long past the time when a company would spend two or three years developing a solution before testing it or delivering it to the market. Change goes so fast that so much can happen in just two to three years. Now, implementations are done in a matter of months. The world has switched to agile developments done in small iterations that are continuously expanded.

HYBRID-SYSTEM DEVELOPMENT

A business may decide to create part of its technology and use third-party solutions to integrate with and create their custom infrastructure. We refer to that as hybrid technology. There are so many possibilities that I could not enumerate them. In fact, hybrid systems are now the type of system that can be found in a majority of organizations—large, medium, or small. The most successful interfaces and systems are the ones offering the best integration options.

OFF-THE-SHELF SYSTEMS AND NETSOURCING

In using technology, the options are renting, paying on a use basis, or buying an existing solution, or some combination of these. There are also companies in the same industry that group together and either create, invest in, or acquire a technology company to deliver technology services and innovation for them. We have seen that in the banking industry in the past, but now, it is seen in the automotive industry. The acquired technology company delivers customized solutions to each partner. Then each business of the coalition can further customize their solutions in house, if needed, and innovate further.

ADVANTAGES AND DISADVANTAGES OF THE DIFFERENT TECHNOLOGY CHOICES

	Own technology	**Off the shelf**	**Hybrid**
Advantages	• Custom creation	• Saves implementation time • More affordable	• Saves time • Better customization • Reduced cost
Disadvantages	• Requires more resources • Higher cost • May be more time consuming	• Less customization • May not be innovative or competitive in some cases	• Integration may be challenging • Incompatibilities may be encountered

TECHNOLOGY NEEDS OR SOLUTIONS FOR DIGITAL TRANSFORMATION

Here is a summary of different technology needs that a business or organization may consider as they think about investing in technology for digital transformation.

- Business Intelligence (data science and solutions)
  - data gathering
  - data cleanup

  - o data analytics
  - o AI
- Mobility
  - o data capture and exchange wherever they are
  - o sensors, smartphones, cameras, GPS, computers
- Business-processing capacity and storage (cloud computing)
  - o data storage, processing, and security
- Business processes digitalization
  - o marketing
  - o delivery options
  - o HR services
  - o sales
  - o vendor management
  - o customer service and management
  - o financial management
  - o administrative services
  - o logistics
  - o resources management
  - o access control and security
  - o design and production
  - o communication (including social community management)
- Process automation
- Organization alignment (digitally enabled)
- Access and security
  - o building access, system access, general security awareness, and enforcement

LEVERAGING AND TRIMMING THE EXISTING TECHNOLOGY

The best technology system is one that is well connected, integrated, and efficient. Every business deserves to have a technology system that is kept up to date and where all infrastructure and solutions can be pinpointed easily. In the past few decades, many companies have used an increasing number of technical systems and solutions that are not always recorded in their technical and business architecture and sometimes not even used. Sometimes different business departments use different systems for a similar function, simply because of personal or business-unit preference, while either of the two systems would have fulfilled both departments' needs.

There is also the case where a system was limited before but now offers more options and is capable of satisfying more business needs. With the digital age, it is important to have easy and quick information flowing. Therefore, integrating systems, platforms, and solutions for easy data retrieval and analysis is a must. When applicable, it is best to use one system instead of two similar ones. That is more cost efficient as well, because a company will save on maintenance, training, and hosting.

Make an inventory of the different technology needs per department, and then combine them for a master document. Use the technology matrix below.

TECHNOLOGY INVENTORY AND OPTIMIZATION MATRIX

Tools/Department	ERP 1	ERP 2	CRM 1	CRM 2	Other/Specify
Human Resources					
Data Science & Business intelligence					
Processing Capacity and Storage (cloud)					
Mobility & IoT					
Process Automation					

Tools/Department	ERP 1	ERP 2	CRM 1	CRM 2	Other/Specify
Digital Business Processing					
Access and security					
Automation					
Organization Alignment					
Other					
Marketing & Sales					
Data Science & Business intelligence					
Processing Capacity and Storage (cloud)					
Mobility & IoT					
Process Automation					
Digital Business Processing					
Access and security					
Automation					
Organization Alignment					
Other					
IT					
Data Science &					
Business intelligence					
Processing Capacity and Storage (cloud)					
Mobility & IoT					
Process Automation					
Digital Business Processing					
Access and security					
Automation					
Organization Alignment					
Other					
Customer Services					
Data Science & Business intelligence					
Processing Capacity and Storage (cloud)					

Tools/Department	ERP 1	ERP 2	CRM 1	CRM 2	Other/Specify
Mobility & IoT					
Process Automation					
Digital Business Processing					
Access and security					
Automation					
Organization Alignment					
Other					
Production					
Data Science & Business intelligence					
Processing Capacity and Storage (cloud)					
Mobility & IoT					
Process Automation					
Digital Business Processing					
Organization Alignment					
Other					

You may repeat the above matrix for as many departments/services as there are in your organization and wherever applicable. Don't hesitate to customize it with specific lists of business processes and functions on the left for each department. The sheet can be used for reviewing existing systems or for choosing new systems.

BEFORE TECHNOLOGY TRANSFORMATION

There is evidence that technology processes are frequently unwritten and done informally in many organizations. Because of that lack of logs or information, we use system-monitoring tools to find out what technical processes are running. It may be a file transfer, a messaging process, data encryption/decryption, conversion, and so forth. This alone can cause us to lose much time in implementing new technology. The lack of knowledge about the existence of hidden technical processes has caused many failures during system implementing, moving, and automating. Sometimes all it takes is a technical map.

By all means, for systems that lack accurate and updated documentation, put a monitoring system in place before making any change to the system. That way, you know the processes and risks involved better.

STANDARDIZATION IS BUSINESS ALIGNMENT

For entire services, service-management procedures and tools should be defined, kept up to date, and followed.

For project-management entities, project management methods and tools should be standardized and used throughout the organization.

Implementing the digital strategy is not to be done in a restrictive silo, but the whole organization should benefit from it. Therefore, it is always important to keep the effects of digital transformation on the whole organization in sight. Of course, there are exceptions to the rules, and that is where access control becomes more relevant.

Optimizing information sharing with the right team/service at the right time and by different means forms the basis for achieving efficiency, better products, and service delivery. It's the basis for automation.

Every implementation should consider the impact on the whole organization, as in the following digital transformation roadmap illustration. Regardless of department, unit, or service names, they all facilitate delivery, and ultimately, success.

Information technology systems should help each of them accomplish their tasks and interact with them all, while considering access security and privacy.

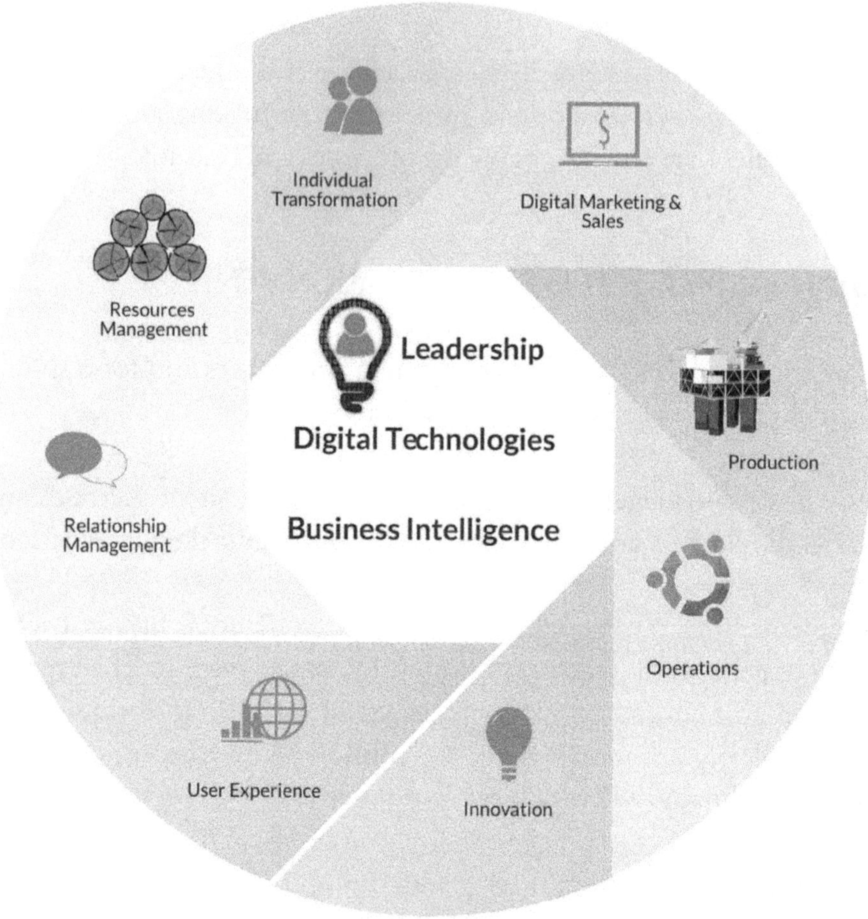

The Digital Transformation Roadmap

The Digital Transformation Success Formula
www.thedigitaltransformationleaders.com

The above is all additional information that will contribute to completing the end-to-end strategic planning done previously.

AUTOMATING FOR COST REDUCTION AND EFFICIENCY

One of the most efficient aspects of digital transformation is cost and error reduction achieved through automation in various parts of the business. However, this efficiency is only for well-understood and well-rounded business or technical processes. Any system or process that is running on a "trial-and-error basis" should avoid automation. In such cases, automation will be a costly and ineffective strategy.

Before, automation tools were expensive, and there were fewer integration options with them. Now, with artificial intelligence, data science, and the Internet of Things, we live in a virtual automation world, and it is accessible and affordable to any person and any business. This alone creates a revolution that takes people out of their comfort zone, to rise above themselves, while also causing fear and desperation for others.

Automation and robotics require great business and technical understanding and mastery to be set up correctly. Knowledge of the automation tool comes in second position. Though automation and robotics may allow us to replace some jobs, it does not replace our brains but merely reproduces and repeats our logical thinking and output. Artificial intelligence is manufactured by humans, and it performs tasks that are more challenging for humans, though some menial tasks are automated as well. Therefore, in setting up automation strategies, it is essential to have in place systems monitoring, alarms, and intervention procedures. A disaster-recovery plan and procedure are also essential, with or without automation.

SUMMARY

Here are some rules for digital-technology implementation success.

The technology system must be:

- time efficient;
- compatible with most other technology;
- suitable for integration;
- shareable;
- of good quality;
- in line with business or organizational strategy
- business focused; and
- adopted into the organization.

TAKING ACTIONS!

1. List your organization's business goals for the next year or two, and assign a priority level to each goal. Then list separately each technology goal necessary for achieving the business goal.
2. Analyze and fill in a Technology Inventory and Optimization Matrix for the unit you are responsible for. Where there is no service for a business service or process in any of the tools listed, mark the related cell in red. That way you see the areas that are lacking. You may customize the form, adding more lines for business functions.
3. Based on the Technology Inventory, analyze what other solutions are missing and the tools that you can bring onboard or that are needed.
4. Decide, in collaboration with your leadership team, the system type you want (off the shelf, customized, hybrid).

CHAPTER ELEVEN

Digital Transformation vs. Data Science

War is 90% information.

— Napoleon Bonaparte

Napoleon understood the real value of data. More than ever, data has become a science in its own right, and we are learning so much about its power. Data is the new currency, and many businesses do not yet understand its value and what their data is telling them about their business. Business intelligence has become sharper.

Here I will approach the basics of data.

Data is one of the main pillars of digital transformation. Data allows us, beyond other things, to analyze, automate, and make informed decisions quickly. Businesses and organizations would not exist without data. Digital transformation has much to do with data capture, processing, analysis, exchange, storage, and access. Further, relevant data empowers business intelligence. This chapter shows the importance of data in digital transformation—how to get it, what to get, and where—and why one should take the best advantage of it.

You don't have to hire a data scientist before taking advantage of data or devising your data strategy. The following will help you make the right decisions about your strategy and implementation plan before hiring a data scientist.

DATA USAGE AND IMPORTANCE

Why do we need data? Let me count the "whys" of how data helps with business transformation. We can use data to:

1. improve business performance in general;
2. create new business models;
3. market and sell better;
4. reduce production time and cost;
5. reduce test costs;
6. reduce error margins;
7. compete and position the business better on the market;
8. gain new customers;
9. keep existing customers;
10. improve customer service to be more efficient;
11. reduce delivery costs;
12. reduce delivery time;
13. improve process flow;

14. anticipate the client's needs;
15. deliver better solutions to consumers;
16. deliver the greatest solution (integrated) packages and more value for the money;
17. prevent fraud and protect rights and value;
18. if fraud happens, find the responsible person(s);
19. pinpoint risk and apply contingencies;
20. innovate;
21. make better hiring decisions;
22. make the best purchases; and
23. make the best technology choices.

And the list could go on and on.

THE DATA THAT ALLOW SUCH OPPORTUNITIES

We have principally two types of data—small data and big data. Small data is the everyday information that we collect or research from prospects/clients/customers with the intent of using it for multiple business purposes. This data is generally organized, structured, and malleable. We use query functions in general to get the information we want from small data. I am talking about the multiple Excel sheets and other small and large databases that we generally have in our organizations.

Big data itself is an accumulation of a vast amount of data not specifically gathered for a purpose. According to the Gartner definition in their IT glossary, "Big data is high-volume, high-velocity, and/or high-variety information assets that demand cost-effective, innovative forms of information processing that enable enhanced insight, decision-making, and process automation."

The dataset in big data is so voluminous that our traditional query, processing, analysis, and storage tools are powerless. Therefore, big data requires specific digital technology to handle it effectively in order to benefit from it.

While big data is very trendy, for your digital transformation, start with small data before going further with big data. The good news for your data strategy is that you can take advantage of digital technologies and data analytics to make better use of small data today than just the good old query functions. But before we go into data analytics, let's see which types of data you need to start your data strategy with small data.

SMALL DATA FOR YOUR DATA STRATEGY

Every industry is different and must explore the types of data that can facilitate business at any or all levels. However, for every business involving customers, market, production, delivery, and finances, these areas give us plenty of types of data we can collect directly or indirectly. Furthermore, each of the above areas has a dependency on the others and on other business areas; therefore, they have information that we share in the process. The type of information we need is information that can allow us to question business processes and improve them in whatever way possible.

The mindset would be, how does having this type of information allow me to take action that will make my business/organization vision a reality? How would having information *X* allow me to improve *Y*? It's about seeing the information in context in, for example, customer information and outside of its context, making a new business model.

Ask how the information would allow me to:

- innovate
- reduce production costs while maintaining effectiveness
- improve processes
- create new business opportunities
- sell more
- gain new markets
- increase ROI
- make better offers to clients
- make better business investments

COLLECTING DATA FOR YOUR BUSINESS AND GOALS

Here is a list of the types of small data you may want to collect and that you can use in your data strategy for business information. Keep in mind the legal aspects of all data you collect. You do not want to go against people's legal right to privacy.

1. Lifestyle data
   a. real-time activities
   b. activities and interests
   c. passion
   d. everyday lifestyle and habits

2. Relationships, organizations, and communities
   a. families
   b. businesses
   c. location
   d. acquaintances and networks

3. Causes that engage people
   a. religious

   b. political
   c. humanitarian
   d. patriotic
   e. situations

4. Business productions and needs
   a. general business needs
   b. professional needs
   c. family needs
   d. innovation needs
   e. wins and fails
   f. positioning and competitiveness
   g. collaborative information
   h. business-process information
   i. business collaborations
   j. professional solutions
   k. professional services

METHODS FOR COLLECTING DATA EFFECTIVELY

We can collect data ourselves, as well as buy it from external sources. In digital marketing, however, collected data is more powerful than purchased data.

Here are some ways to collect data. The most used way of collecting data is with opt-in forms through one or more of the following:

1. Targeted giveaways or lead magnets
2. Webinars
3. Surveys
4. Quizzes

5. Drafts, competitions, or awards
6. Community sharing
7. Social-media actions (invitations, shares, quizzes, games, surveys)
8. Live networking
9. On-site gathering and lead collecting
10. Mobile marketing (phone, app, SMS, GPS campaigns, etc.)
11. Partnership and multiple types of collaborations
12. Online searches
13. Purchasing (ad campaigns, pay per clicks, etc.)
14. Collect from clients during purchase or other interaction online
15. Using artificial intelligence tools
16. Bought from third parties and generated using specialized tools

DATA-PROTECTION PRIVACY AND LEGAL REMINDERS

Always make sure that the data is collected in a legal way, and inform people about your privacy policy, or make it available to them. Since laws vary from one place to another, consult with your business' jurisdiction and other places where you are doing business. For instance, you may be allowed to collect some data from a source but may be required to inform the source you are collecting data and the specific purpose.

Be sure to know what you can and cannot do with the data collected for your business, especially the rules when it comes to storage and fraud prevention. This is especially true for sensitive data related to individuals' health, finances, and personal lives. There are different rules for different industries, so check the rules for your industry.

Due to new regulations constantly coming out as innovation progresses, it is best to have someone dedicated to monitoring legal changes in regions where you do business.

PROCESSING AND STORING DATA

The digital age opened the way to a new way of storing and processing data—the cloud! Cloud computing revolutionizes storage and processing, making obsolete server rooms, mainframes, towers, and computer-storage devices all at once. But the real treats consist of the data mobility, affordability, increased capacity, and fast processing speed.

Some people will add security as another treat, but that is still up for debate because, like in life, nothing is perfect, and there is often a price to pay. Security is reinforced, and professionals are working hard on it and creating wonders. However, security does not depend only on the systems but also on the people who use the systems.

Our data use has increased tremendously with our social lifestyles and digital technology formats. Imagine that every country had a medium or long list of radio and TV stations, printed press, and newspapers. Today almost every individual and every business in the civilized world has the potential to be, and most are, at once, a radio, TV station, printing press, and newspaper, thanks to social media such as YouTube, Facebook, Twitter, Periscope, Google Hangout, basic e-mailing (Gmail)—and you name it. Our banking and our payments are done mostly digitally and are done this way for most public or private administration in every field or industry. That is a gigantic load of data being processed daily.

Companies such as Google and Amazon have made large data storage accessible and affordable to individuals and their households globally. This is just like how Microsoft made the personal computer available and Apple made smartphones available. Whether it is a pay-as-you-go system or reserves of a certain capacity, small and large businesses can easily find the right service for them according to their needs and their bank accounts. Find what's right for your organization, your business, or you name it—but don't run to do these steps just yet—not before reading about data analytics below.

MIGRATING DATA TO THE CLOUD

Once a decision is reached to move data to the cloud, then, although this is a technology-focused project between you and your data leaders, your organization and clients want this operation to happen without them noticing. Migrating data is risky, especially for old data systems, due to lack of information of all the exchanges that take place. I am not discussing platform compatibility here, but I am recommending a few things:

1. Auditing and monitoring

Before any data migration takes place, put in place a system for recording and monitoring data processing, so that all data links and exchanges can be identified and the migration plan can be effective.

2. Security during migration

Migration is a sensitive time for fraud. Extra care should be taken both for physical access and digital access to the system.

3. Backup

Always have backup copies of whatever data is being manipulated.

4. Rollback procedures

Always have rollback procedures well defined, step by step, in case the desired results are not achieved, or in more challenging cases, you can roll back to the previous situation until you sort out bigger challenges.

5. Phasing Data Migration

Take care to migrate data in well-defined business phases and not altogether.

Make sure to have a great service-delivery agreement with the cloud provider that covers your organization's interest in terms of support, availability, disaster recovery, processing capacity, security, specific services with their frequencies, accountabilities, and such.

DATA ANALYTICS AND BUSINESS INTELLIGENCE

You can benefit from your data using the good old query functionalities. But allow me to introduce you to another world of possibilities with data analytics. I promise that data analytics can help you benefit gigantically with your small data. We are speaking about taking advantage of true business intelligence using your data, the right technological tools, and genuine business intellect.

In order to benefit from your data as above, you will need the right business-analytics tools to process your data according to well-defined criteria. There are many business-analytics solutions on the market that would allow you to interpret your business data. Having a dashboard configured with critical information about business or technology performance allows leaders to make the right decisions and take the right actions for business success.

In the process of writing this part about data analytics, I reached out to my friend, former classmate, business-intelligence specialist, and expert in data analytics and business intelligence, Sergei Peleshuk. Our discussion gave me more insights into data analytics and business-intelligence possibilities so that I could simplify the approach for you.

THERE ARE THREE TYPES OF DATA ANALYTICS FOR BUSINESS USE:

Descriptive Analytics. This is a type of historic or log-based data that uses aggregation and data mining to deliver insight into the past and reveal what happened. The lessons learned allow us to do better in the future.

Predictive Analytics. It uses statistical models and forecast techniques to understand progression and predict what could happen in the future under various circumstances. That way, we can create contingency plans and improve risk management.

Prescriptive Analytics. It uses data optimization and simulation algorithms to identify possible outcomes and provide advice on the best actions to take for a given situation.

Several technologies exist to easily create dashboards for better use of data analytics. However, to get the best out of the technology and data, you need sharp business intelligence to identify the main outcomes you'll need for better decision-making and to define the logic or program for the desired outcome on your fancy dashboard. This is where the genius of your business-intelligence specialist can save you worries, headaches, and poor decision-making that could undermine your business goals or at least cause delays.

Another technology that makes data analytics and business intelligence sharper is the Internet of Things, or IoT. Thanks to the Internet of Things, sensors, scanners, and GPS devices can record, scan, and transmit crucial data. This data can then be processed automatically using digital-automation tools, another disruptive technology that facilitates data analytics. Sequences can then be created for the chain of things connected together using the internet and automated to behave according to specific programming. Thanks to capturing this data and processing it, errors can be reduced, costs can be reduced, and decision-making can be improved, and business can act directly where needed, at the right time. With the right data analytics, you can say good-bye to poor guesses, indecision, delayed information, long waits, sudden bad surprises, and doubt. Risk management precision is improved with data analytics.

In a context where everything is changing inside and outside the organization, data analytics is of tremendous value in allowing us to anticipate, understand, and respond to different situations.

While the business intelligence and/or data specialist creates the right dashboard for your monitoring purpose, it is you, the leader, who must decide what information matter most to you. Beware of falling into the trap of monitoring everything and finally becoming overwhelmed due to lack of priority. Your first priority before monitoring is to know what information/process/business flow you need to monitor to make a difference for your business or unit.

BIG DATA AND DIGITAL TRANSFORMATION

Now that we've seen "small data" as small-scale data that you intentionally capture to improve the business, let's approach the large-scale data that we can use for business transformation—big data.

Big data appears scary to many because of its giant size and massive needs for processing. Big data is data collected at any given time that is not intended for a specific purpose but can find many purposes. The volume of data exchanged online in a matter of days across the world through social media, for example, is amazingly big. That is part of the data that contributes to big data.

Processing big data effectively requires capacity that our home computers do not have in general, despite the greatest improvements in this area. One of the challenges of big data is that it is messy. The great news is that there are more and more tools on the market that can make sense of it.

Like we did above with the small-data approach, we must first determine the goals we have for using big data. From business improvement, innovation, and creating a new business model, determine what you want to achieve with your business strategy. Then big data can be used to achieve that goal.

Digital transformation implies making use of both small data and big data. Don't be scared by big data, but use the tools and specialized solutions that allow you to make the most of it.

Find out what your competitors are doing with big data to have a better understanding of the innovation taking place in your industry. Analyze as well what kind of information could improve or even revolutionize your industry. Research the tools used in your industry and where the focus is. (Visit my website, digitaltransformationleaders.com, for all that.)

Here is a very simple analogy for making use of big data. Imagine that you had a huge pile of messy and unmatched socks to make use of. You would want to start searching for and matching socks that are in good shape, not too funny-looking, and maybe in specific sizes. So you would be cleaning up, matching, sorting, trashing, and even recycling. That's the same for big data, except that it is so huge that you couldn't do it manually. Like small data, there are many technologies that will help make sense of big data by cleaning, searching for patterns, matching, categorizing, analyzing, interpreting...you name it.

DATA-SCIENCE PROFESSIONS

Data is such a hot asset with so many more possibilities than the profession that spawned the data-scientist profession. Data scientists explore and monetize opportunities within data, especially big data. In their October, 2012, magazine issue, *Harvard Business Review* designated the data scientist as the sexiest job of the twenty-first century.3

According to *Big Data Made Simple*, "A data scientist is a person who has the knowledge and skills to conduct sophisticated and systematic analyses of data. A data scientist extracts insights from data sets for product development and evaluates and identifies strategic opportunities."4

Many other data professions are being bred from data science today, so data is a large part of digital transformation, and every digital transformation strategy must have a data strategy part that includes both small and big data.

Big data strategy is and will continue to be largely a valuable asset for business because it reflects our digital lifestyle. We search online for any information we need before taking actions small or big. We are influenced in our purchases by people we call influencers. We use our smartphones to access multiple information sites through the internet and/or via applications (apps), social media, and email; the smartphone has become our primary way of socializing with others.

To summarize, we now live digital lives. It means that each of us has a digital identity with the possibilities and risks that come with it. Our digital identity has become a great indicator in the world economy. Our digital identities allow business to categorize its clients and prospects in order to produce specifically for that client type, reduce waste, reach out directly, and sell its product to that client, sometimes before even creating the solution. Our digital identity gives business leverage, speed, and intelligence that was less accessible before.

The good thing is that we have fun while creating our digital lives, knowingly or unknowingly making it more accessible to others. Imagine being without your smartphone or computer for a week or two. How would you feel, being disconnected from your social network? Not knowing what is happening and not participating in events? For as long as we enjoy and continue to have a digital footprint, there will be a need to use the footprints we leave to innovate, analyze, gain understanding, and so on.

ALTERNATIVES TO HIRING A DATA SCIENTIST

Startups and small businesses that cannot afford to hire a data scientist can still take advantage of big data. Software like Metamarkets, Tableau, QlikView, KNIME, OpenRefine, RapidMiner, and Google

Fusion and Tables, to name a few, offer ways to gain insight about data for less than the price of hiring a data scientist. You can have your data specialists trained, as well, with the countless continuing education courses offered on data science online or in many learning environments.

SUMMARY

Aside from technology and leadership, data is one of the main pillars of digital transformation. One of the digital economy's main asset is data because everyone—and now progressively everything—has a digital identity. Your digital strategy should take into account these digital identities and the opportunities they represent to make the best of it. Short-, medium-, and long-term data strategy will enrich your digital transformation strategy, producing the greatest insights and the best return on investment and inspiring some of the greatest innovations.

TAKING ACTIONS!

1. Define what small data you already have and how your organization is taking advantage of it.
2. Is there any additional small data you could collect? How can you collect it?
3. What is your data storage and processing strategy? Is your organization using the cloud only or a mix of cloud and your own storage? Is there any foreseen data migration to plan and execute?
4. Do you want to use Big Data and what for? Define the goals that the business wants to achieve using Big Data.

5. What tools are you using to interpret data? Can they be improved or changed altogether?
6. What kind of dashboard would be valuable for business decisions for different business units?
7. What data skills are necessary based on your organization's situation? What other skills are not needed anymore?
8. Create your data strategy with the support of your data- and business-intelligence leader(s) while focusing on achieving your organization goals.

CHAPTER TWELVE

Process Streamlining for Effectiveness

I put my heart and my soul into my work and have lost my mind in the process.

— VINCENT VAN GOGH

Process is "the how" in getting things done, and digital transformation allows us to reevaluate process to get better efficiency. Some processes will be either upgraded, modified, or suppressed, while new ones are being created. Since digital transformation allows the creation of new business models and new business approaches, streamlining and creating new processes is a major task in the transformation process. Reviewing processes for effectiveness requires a great business understanding and an understanding of the "why" of each process and subprocess.

PROCESS IMPROVEMENT OPTIONS

As we review processes in the organization, be they business or technical processes, we have one or more of the following options.

1. Process Creation

Creating new processes may be necessary because either new business models were identified or because old processes became completely or mostly irrelevant. It happens often for new delivery models and new value creations. Imagination is the limit to process creation. As for any new creation, the determining factor is its "why?" In other words, what value does this process bring directly or indirectly? What does it facilitate? Is it worth the investment in time or effort? Is there any disadvantage to the new process? How important is it, and should something be done about it?

2. Process Elimination

Some business processes may become obsolete because of completely different ways of working. We may choose to cancel them.

However, we should verify if a transition period is needed. If so, the transition period is the time to communicate the process cancellation or change, inform people of the new option, and allow people to migrate smoothly to the new process or way of working, leading up to the chosen cancellation date.

3. Process Enhancement

Process enhancement allows us to improve an existing process by first acknowledging what assets are still useful and which parts are no longer relevant or effective. The part that is not relevant may then either be updated, improved with a tool, automated, or discarded.

4. Process Integration or Realignment

Two or more processes may be integrated or combined for better flow and effectiveness. In that case, all possible impacts should be analyzed for every possible dependency of each process as well as all subprocesses (if there are any). Every impact should then be addressed with contingencies provided.

5. Process Automation

Processes can be automated using an automation tool, and only stable and well-tested processes should be automated. For any unstable process, time should be invested in making it reliable before automating it. Also, the logical process should be clear and written before automation. A mistake many teams new to automation make is poor contingency planning. Make sure that the risk of malfunctions at different levels of the process is covered. Malfunctions (or unexpected intrusions/dysfunctions) should generate a warning or an alarm, and an action plan must be clearly defined for that. Furthermore, a responsible person (owner) and a backup person should be designated at all times.

6. Process Outsourcing

Less frequently, a process may be outsourced. In that case, some parameters must be clearly defined and agreed upon between both parties. The parameters may vary for different sectors, but a Terms of Service or a Service Agreement document must be defined as a base, with at least the following information: entry criteria, exit criteria, process duration, compensation, risk and contingencies, accountability, and legal information.

For each business and technical process in the organization, analyzing and implementing the above options for transformation result in great improvements that translate into higher ROI, plus employee and customer satisfaction. Use the matrix below to complete a concise inventory and adjust it to your situation or the area that is applicable to you, or every unit under your authority.

PROCESS-TRANSFORMATION INVENTORY MATRIX

Transformation Processes	Enhancement	Elimination	Creation	Integration	Automation	Outsourcing
HR Processes						
Process A						
Process B						
Process C						
……						
Marketing & Sales Processes						
Process A						
Process B						
Process C						
……						
Technical Processes						
Process A						
Process B						
Process C						
……						
Customer Services Processes						
Process A						
Process B						

Transformation Processes	Enhancement	Elimination	Creation	Integration	Automation	Outsourcing
Process C						
……						
Production Process						
Process A						
Process B						
Process C						
……						
QA & Test Processes						
Process A						
Process B						
Process C						
……						
Financial Processes						
Process A						
Process B						
Process C						
……						

PROCESS-TRANSFORMATION ADOPTION AND USE

Having new processes and process owners does not guarantee that they will be used or followed in the organization. Countless organizations have invested millions in new methods, processes, and tools that become just more papers collecting dust on shelves and drawers. You don't want that. This is something that happens unconsciously when, as human beings, we automatically go back to our old way of working, as it is deeply recorded in our subconscious minds. The goal now is to erase the old process and imprint on our brains the new processes or workstyles, so that we adopt the new processes unconsciously.

Here are a few considerations for better adoption and use of the transformed processes. The following are applicable for employees within the organization and, in some cases, for customers.

1. Involve the team in brainstorming sessions about the processes. Their experience using these processes is priceless and can lead to great innovation.
2. Have role-play and timed games around the processes as in real business situations. Take advantage of that to organize an event small or big—you decide.
3. Have a poll around a specific process.
4. Analyze previous complaints and the effectiveness of processes.
5. Have a competition for the best process improvement or creation where applicable in your organization or for customers to participate, and reward the best propositions.
6. After a process has been implemented, have a competition ongoing for the most effective use of a process.
7. Have memorable signs or items that remind one of the new processes on the organization's premises, on networked computers, or, in some cases, on people's individual desks.
8. Test, monitor, and improve processes where necessary.

SUMMARY

Business processes will be reengineered during digital transformation and most likely several times. Don't think that because you change or adjust a business process the previous year, it can't be changed the following year. The process is how we do things and, with the speed of innovation and smart technologies' availability, we should do a regular inventory and evaluation of our processes for business effectiveness. While processes are important, stay attached to business goals but not to business processes. Artificial intelligence, with its multiple disciplines, is one key digital technology that helps boost processes today, and things can and do change fast. Remember that even in automated processes, human monitoring and adjustment are necessary.

TAKING ACTIONS!

1. Using the chart above, make an inventory of the different departments, business units, services, projects, programs, and/or processes applicable to your role. Analyze the situation for each in collaboration with your team or alone, according to your situation. Customize the inventory sheet according to your situation.
2. Involve leaders but also have users involved in the transformation, as specified in the Process-Transformation Adoption and Use section above. Create a test and monitor the procedures, followed by a review and improvement action for each process.

CHAPTER THIRTEEN

Enabling the Digital Organization

They have in me struck down but the trunk of the tree for the freedom of black men and women; the roots are many and deep—they will shoot up again!

— TOUSSAINT LOUVERTURE

The digitally enabled organization is one of the best investments for a sustainable transformation. Transformation leaders create more leaders. While many are predicting the disappearance of the organization, organizations that are made to last will keep investing in people. While technology is a major investment for digital transformation, investing in people remains the best investment for digital transformation. However, our vision about the organization as it is today must change. Without the right mindset, leadership, and attitude, all the investment in technology and time to create the transformation can be wasted. In fact, most project failures, regardless of their industry, are caused by human-related issues. Even when a technology failure is highlighted, it is often traced back to the human cause or error. Technology does not correct human error if it was not programmed to. Humans create technology, and humans correct technology errors and learn to rise above them, not the other way around. Regardless of the transformed reality, technology cannot replace humans, and therefore organizations will always need people.

AN UNMATCHED AND UNDERUSED ASSET

Digital transformation is not a "one-time" initiative or project, but a constant journey to transform the business and perform in the transformed organization. Many organizations use digital transformation as a way to reduce costs by firing employees, automating their business, and outsourcing what they can where they find the best value. While this may be in some places an effective cost-reduction strategy, it is not a long-term success strategy.

Some people predict the disappearance of the employee status and organizations alike, but this prediction neglects one undisputable fact—that is, the human brain is unmatched and unreplaceable so far. What we replace is the use of a small portion of that asset as we know it. I see it as an end of a phase and a start of another. The other requires more innovation from all of us.

The businesses that implement the organizational strategy for digital transformation described in this chapter are the ones becoming one or all of the following:

- disruptors
- innovators
- dominators
- holistic transformers

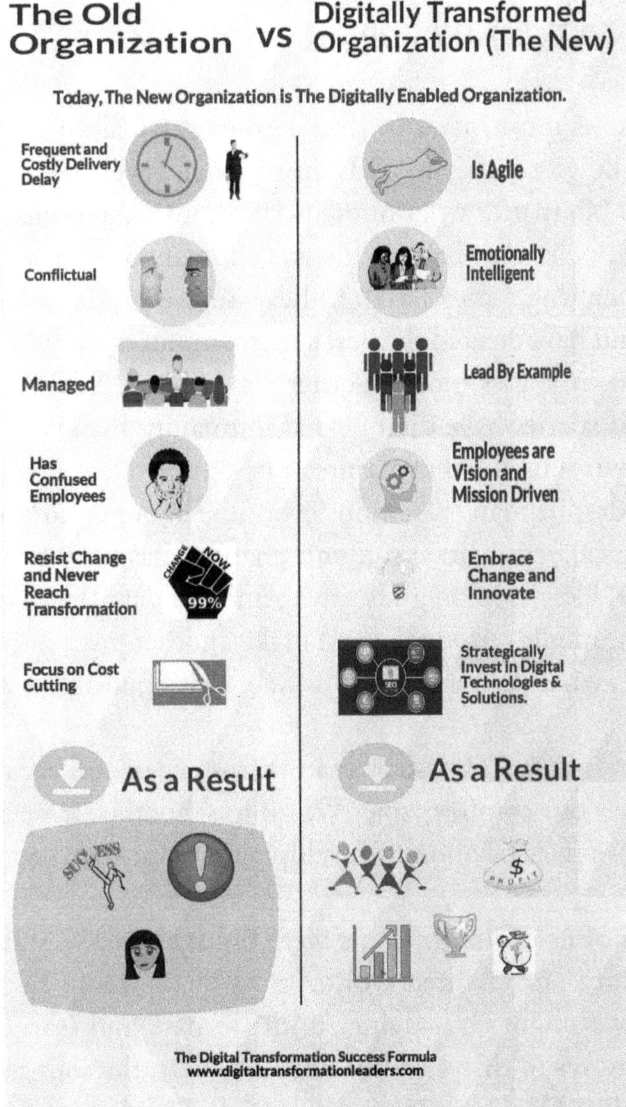

The other businesses left after these four categories may keep adjusting to change, postponing the inevitable, or surviving as long as they can until they die or they are cannibalized by the company types listed above.

SMARTER RAW MATERIAL MEANS BETTER OPPORTUNITY FOR ALL

Organizations must invest in their resources (small or large) because that is the best asset they have! To justify that, I will go back to prehistoric time. No matter what humans faced, no matter what version of history you believe to be true for you, humans have always survived whatever challenges they faced. Otherwise, we would not exist today. We exist and have created the best supercomputers. People make technology and machines, not the other way around. While many plant and animal species have disappeared, humanity has overcome everything thrown at us either by nature or by our own fabrication. The human race, despite many variations over time in our culture and beliefs, plus biological, social, and economic changes, has survived and moved to new eras, like the night gives way to another day. The next day is full of opportunities for us to take and make another piece of history. The question is, what do we want to make of that opportunity?

The fears, worries, and despair many of us experience are normal because we left our comfort zone. We go to school, become professionals, and work in association to develop our community and our world.

If a bunch of us civilized people were brought to a wild jungle with nothing from our civilized world, most of us would be helpless at first, and we might start dying, until we dare and learn to survive and create ways to thrive or live normally with the sources available. Several reality TV shows entertain us with this idea, except that they don't go as far as leaving people to die or be transformed, though the easier experience has still transformed many participants in their thinking and lifestyles already.

Today, we see many of our situations changing, but we also have more resources available than ever before. The resources we have today are the new raw materials for creating greater things. Improved resources do not replace our people; our raw materials just got smarter.

If you observe mindfully, you will see that, like our raw materials, we have become smarter as well. There have been so many changes happening so fast, that we have become more mentally fit and experienced to face the transformation. Even our children appear to evolve faster than their parents. I remember when pregnant with my first son, I bought an audio program to wear on my stomach daily to train his brain. Only later, I got to learn more about brain science and how we program our brain consciously and unconsciously daily.

OUR TWO OPTIONS—TRANSFORMATION OR DEATH

Today we have two options, and whether we make a decision or not, one of these options will become our reality.

1. *Losing.* We fight, cry, and resist the transformation, or we do nothing. In that case, it will be a new day regardless, and we die without taking advantage of the opportunities.
2. *Winning.* We tap into our brain, our experiences, and our resources and evolve to something even greater than what we, the human race, have already created.

In fact, both of the above options will happen. The (mentally) fittest will rush toward option two, even when they have doubts and don't know what they are doing. As digital transformation leaders, I position you in option two. And your role is to brace yourself to get fitter and, as much as possible, try to lead the people who picked option one to transform and unleash their potential, and help them to join you to create the innovations in the newly transformed era, that is, to digitally enable your organization or your team. Organizations that succeed in doing that continuously are the ones that are made to last.

There are several things to do in order to facilitate continuous digital transformation in our organizations.

- Leaders must grow and transform themselves so they can lead in challenging situations.
- They must seize opportunities to innovate and thrive in their industries or sectors.
- They must help their remaining individuals or employees to fly higher by shifting their mindset to embrace a transformed workstyle dominated by constant change, disruption, and innovation, regardless of their age.
- They must stay aware or be on top of multiple smart resources available to them as raw materials for better efficiency.

SELF-TRANSFORMATION

I spoke about self-transformation for digital leaders in Chapter 1. To help transform others, we must start with self-transformation and lead by example.

RELEASING GIANTS

The most critical investments that one should make right away, even before starting digital transformation itself, concern the organization. Many see the first step as firing employees. Firing is equal to the deaths of people's mindsets. Firing results in people living with a negative mindset, filled with uncertainty, fear, doubt, and searching for a purpose worth living for day after day. To me, that leads to depression, despair, disillusion, and maybe even actual death. As a transformational leader, you are called to instead "release giants" so that they can achieve their next project or next life assignment, not fire them. You are supposed to give them a promotion, and it starts with promoting their mindset to achieve their next great thing, whatever it may be. Their next step is out of your scope. From now on, forget about firing. Learn about releasing giants for their next assignment and acknowledging their wings. This is not a done-once process but is part of leading and preparing individuals to grow and helping them be transformed for their next assignment at the end of a cycle.

SEIZING OPPORTUNITIES TO THRIVE IN A TRANSFORMING WORLD

Change and transformation bring pain, and it is the pain that helps transform us by getting us out of our zones of comfort. The next step is the fresh start. Though we may not be aware of it yet, opportunities lie waiting for us to grab them, work on them, and thrive. Though it is not always a straight process, it is just the cycle of life. Sometimes, opportunities come as a threat or are wrapped in sandpaper. Only those who can see beyond the threat can lead the crowd to thrive together. As a transformational leader, you must practice seeing farther than the threat, and that's through visioning, as discussed in Chapter 2.

HELPING YOUR GIANTS TO FLY IN FIVE STEPS

Helping your giants to fly comes down to leading your people to unleash their potential, strengthen all they have, and follow you. But before they can follow you or fly with you, they need your help. You can either give them wings or break their fragile wings. Here are the five steps to digitally enabled your organization and help your giants fly with you.

1. Inspiration

Inspire them with the organization's vision and your own transformation and that of others.

2. Empowerment

Empower them with their mission, the company's values, their roles, and their importance in turning the vision into a reality.

3. Trust

Trust them by giving them more knowledge, responsibilities, power of decision, accountability, and a flat organizational structure.

4. Reward

Rewards include self-rewards and rewards from their leader. Reward them by sharing the success with them, complimenting them for progress, and encouraging and rating them positively toward the desired outcome. Their transformation is the greatest self-reward they could ever experience.

5. Evaluate and Repeat

Evaluate how successful your actions were. Identify the lessons learned, the wins and where improvement could be needed. Then repeat the process for all time in your organization.

Leaders must tap into the organization's culture, business values, individuals' value and individual transformation while implementing the steps above to digitally enable their organization. As a result of implementing these five steps, team performance will increase and the transformation can happen.

Digital Transformation (DT) Win	Digital Death (DD) Lose
Self-transformation	Fight
Releasing giant	Fire
Empowering giant	Do nothing
Transformation	Blame
Innovation	Death

Additional tools to enable organization:

- document management and sharing between groups
- unofficial gatherings for brainstorming or networking
- regular polls and survey and quiz tools

SUMMARY

Organizations that invest in enabling their organization experience a greater return on their digital transformation investment because these organizations become the most innovative, customer focused, engaged, and as a result, successful. A big gap exists between digitally enabled organizations and other organizations fighting the transformation. While the latter are more into blaming, resisting, and protecting their current situations, the digitally enabled organizations are finding opportunities to innovate, grow, lead the way, and thrive. As a result, digitally enabled organizations outrun other organizations and perform better.

TAKING ACTIONS!

1. Identify which of the following business types your organization aims to resemble and brainstorm how it is being expressed. Imagine new possibilities for the chosen business type(s).

    - disruptors
    - innovators
    - dominators
    - holistic transformers

2. Using the five steps to digitally enable your organization, list for each step at least three actions that you can take to transform your organization.
3. Implement at least one action for each of the steps.

CHAPTER FOURTEEN

A True Story About Cost Cutting and Effectiveness

Almost all decisions based on cost accounting are utterly wrong.

— Eliyahu Goldratt

COST CUTTING VS. TRANSFORMATION

Heather let go of the door handle as she walked out of her superior's office, confused and in disbelief. She took a deep breath as if to renew her strength, and she let sink in what was just asked of her. She was asked to submit her plan to reduce by 20 percent her department's budget and still deliver the department's services and ongoing projects for the year.

She looked at Justin, who preceded her from the meeting. Justin received the same assignment. He walked at a slow pace and then turned halfway toward Heather to start a conversation. "How in the world can we make this happen without compromising the many ongoing and high-priority projects? That's not realistic. How are you going to do it, Heather?"

To which Heather answered, "I don't know yet, but what I know is that my team is very busy day after day with short deadlines, and reducing headcount will surely cause more delays in service delivery."

This happened about one year ago. Both Heather and Justin got to work to deliver their assignments.

JUSTIN'S APPROACH

1. Justin submitted his cost-cutting plan for his department on time as requested. The following was a summary of his proposition, which was designed to be fully effective in three months' time. He would let go of three external consultants and then redistribute their work.
2. Five full-time employees would be terminated, and their work would also be redistributed.
3. The priority order of several deliveries would be modified.
4. Most project-delivery dates would be postponed.
5. Extras, such as free access to the coffee machine for the employees, would be suppressed. The vending machines would stay in the building, and employees would pay for their own drinks.
6. Quarterly team activities were to be eliminated.

As a result, Justin's plan would reduce costs by 20 percent in three months, and the delivery schedule would be modified. The plan was accepted and implemented in Justin's department.

HEATHER'S APPROACH

Heather acknowledged that she was operating with only the bare essentials after she had already cut so much during the last five years. So she reached out and asked me if I could help. I then asked Heather to give me more info about the department, their business, and technical operations. We agreed that we needed more time to deliver a sustainable cost-reduction plan. Therefore, Heather negotiated and was granted another month before submitting her plan.

During that time, we reviewed the business and technical processes, the tools used, the organizational structure, the teams, the roles, and the outside collaboration in Heather's department. We worked with the team leaders to find answers for many questions. Together, we analyzed every aspect of her department to create more efficiency throughout.

Her proposition could be summarized as such:

1. Several business processes were to be shortened, improved, or suppressed, and five new business processes were to be created.
2. Three technical processes were to be optimized and then automated.
3. Two positions were to be eliminated, and ten others would be modified.

4. Two services were to make use of one existing tool, instead of the two similar ones they were each using, reducing maintenance cost, licensing fees, and duplicate work.
5. New rules were to be defined for more effectiveness.
6. Coaching sessions were to be delivered to several teams as they adopted the new work approach.

As a result, the department would increase delivery capacity by 15 percent while reducing cost by 18 percent over a six-month period.

Heather's proposition was accepted and implemented for her department.

POST IMPLEMENTATION ONE YEAR LATER

JUSTIN'S DEPARTMENT

Justin had a harsh time implementing the plan in his department, as it caused more stress, conflicts, and dissatisfaction in the organization while decreasing production.

Employee morale went down and has remained there, since there is no improvement to look forward to.

The elimination of free coffee and their quarterly get-together created for the employees an environment of lack, poor recognition, decreased collaboration, and decreased reliability.

The clients were very disappointed with the delayed deliveries. To make matters worse, they experienced a high turnover rate, causing them to be even farther behind in product delivery.

HEATHER'S DEPARTMENT

Heather's department is now running effectively and delivering more, at a faster rate than before, and at a lower cost. In fact, after the implementation and up to the present day, the cost is now reduced by 22 percent.

Cost reduction should be a search for improved effectiveness first. Approaching cost cutting as a search-and-destroy mission to cut all extras or reduce only the immediately apparent costs just decreases productivity, and therefore, ends up costing the company more.

How many processes, tools, and roles are outdated, duplicated, irrelevant, and/or repetitive in our units? How about the ones that no one knows why they exist? Or the multiple tools that our teams use, when just a few of these tools can be used by more or all of the teams? How many manual processes can be automated?

SUMMARY

Cost reduction is costly, but effectiveness is free and rewarding, as it pays for itself with increased productivity. The good news is that each one of us at our own levels can create more effectiveness.

CHAPTER FIFTEEN

Digital Transformation Rescue - Cases Studies

No matter how long you train someone to be brave, you never know if they are or not until something real happens.

— VERONICA ROTH

WHAT IS HAPPENING WITH MY DIGITAL TRANSFORMATION INVESTMENT?

Why is my digital transformation or business transformation not generating a significant return or why it is taking forever and draining our finances?

There are five main reasons why I see organizations struggle with digital transformation, and here I am also providing you with advice on what to do to solve the situations. I use case studies to illustrate them.

1. Transformation with fuzzy vision or no transformative vision
2. Automation without innovation
3. Digital transformation tools chaos
4. Collaborative chaos
5. Low level of leadership and accountability

1. TRANSFORMATION WITH FUZZY VISION OR NO TRANSFORMATIVE VISION

The transformation with fussy vision or no transformative vision is an organization where the governance or the main leader of the company lacks clarity or is not sure of the strategic vision of the organization. This is the capital sin in Digital Transformation. While it is a very negative situation, sometimes we can understand many of these leaders. Some are in cases where they have their hands tied with budget restrictions, an ever-changing digital landscape, lack of qualified talent, global economic challenges, penalizing employee unions, changing governmental regulations, abundant new technologies and technologies vendors soliciting their attention daily, and complete accountability and responsibility for their decisions good or bad. Furthermore, they are human beings like everyone else and are not exempt from any personal challenge that a person may face related to family, health, divorce, the death of a loved one, for example. They are not immune to any internal or external challenges life may throw at a person in a lifetime. There are enough reasons to be confused, worried, or not being in a state of mind that facilitates creating the right vision for an organization.

I have been in situations where, after some technology implementation program, that I was so drained, no grand vision, be it personal or professional, would come out of me before I rejuvenate myself. Life is made of cycles, and one of the first things any executive needs is to create in their agenda, the space to rejuvenate themselves. It should be a part of your program. Everyone needs that, but as an executive, the more people you have in your organization, the more your vision and decisions will affect. So, you have a great responsibility, and to deliver, you need to renew your mind always. The great thing about the digital age is that you can delegate more, exercise more control, and earn more freedom to think higher, innovate, and care for yourself as well.

It is essential to have a transformative vision, and it must be clear.

If you get in your car and start to drive, but you see the vision you have in front of you is that of this picture, do you continue driving, or do you stop and try to get a better view?

I bet that you would try to improve your visibility as much as you could, starting with your car wipers and, if not enough, you'll get off your seat and try developing the visibility as much as you can to take the road. Unless you have a self-driving car that relies on other visibility features, but who knows if the car's visibility features are not altered as well if there has been a severe climate disaster? But, let's stay positive. The sad truth is that many organizations that are implementing digital transformation today are driving without vision, therefore without visibility and many are driving toward digital death with the sole excuse that they have to keep moving as not to be left behind. This is the reason why every executive must clarify their vision for themselves and the organization that they are leading.

The car visibility analogy is the same for the company vision. If it is not clear for the executives who have a front seat, it will be even foggier for others in the organization, and for them, it will be even more complicated because they don't have a front view like executives do. As a result, there will be more fear, more conflict, powerful resistance, self-protection, no trust, no loyalty, and no organizational support.

I am sure that you see the problems you'll be facing from all that.

You can prevent that and use your energy for innovation! In Chapter 3, I help you create your transformative vision.

MEET TONY FROM CORP 1

Meet Tony, an executive for a leading home appliance manufacturer who has been transforming their business.

Corp 1 starts digital transformation because the competition is transforming, and they don't want to be left behind. They started transformation by imitating what they saw competitors doing in the market, in general, to keep up. They implemented a social media strategy, developed some apps, and implemented a few strategies so they could stay relevant and make some noises at certain moments.

Corp 1 objectives were scattered over their business divisions, and they did not have any specific competitive advantage compared to their competitors.

As a result of misalignments in the organization and especially in the business units where a few transformation projects were taking place, the projects were delayed continuously, rephased, and sometimes abandoned. Things were slow-moving in the organization and large sums of money were being poured into some projects that were repetitively rephrased or that were soon overtaken by changes in the market. The executives had had enough of not seeing positive ROI in the company and technology projects that were not delivering. When they blamed suppliers for not delivering, the suppliers blamed them back, saying that they were not clear in what they wanted or did not provide them the requested resources. Corp 1's clients began leaving. Corp 1 was in big trouble and needed to turn things around fast to keep their position in the market in the short-term and medium-term gain more market share.

Then they contacted yours truly, M. Nadia Vincent, after change management and leadership seminar that one of their leaders heard at a global professional event. In about a month and after a few work sessions, I had delivered a new strategic approach and later, a new roadmap to implement and transform their business. Fortunately, they did act fast in implementing the roadmap, and soon, their strategic vision had become a reality, first by maintaining their position and eight months later by going after more market share.

What I helped Corp 1 implement in their roadmap:

1. Define a new, clarified vision for the company and its executives
2. Improve the transformation leadership team.
3. Create a unique customer experience.
4. Improved employee experience.
5. Engage in new partnerships that will help them deliver innovative solutions that align with their strategic vision, and faster, to their client.

6. Create a unique competitive advantage and get the market engaged with that.
7. Review their project management approach and delivery method to the point of delivering projects that were stagnating and eliminating projects that were not going to bring significant value to the organization or that were doomed to fail.
8. Align the different parts of the organization and prepare them to contribute to the transformation instead of restraining it.
9. Help employees redefine their personal and career goals and align them with the organization's success.

This is the power of a clear and innovative strategic digital transformation vision. It reveals the flaws at every corner in the business, and with the right corrective actions, you can turn the company around to a success story.

2. AUTOMATION WITHOUT INNOVATION

Clearly said, if you are automating the business, meaning replacing humans with machines, that is not innovation. If that is all you offer, either the customer will look elsewhere, or your employees will resist the transformation, and the organization will experience conflicts both internally and externally.

Automation is only one aspect of the many facets of digital transformation; it is not transformation by itself.

In every transformation, we must measure the advantages we gain in the transformation. It may be that it allows the company to maintain its position on the market. But that is not enough, the transformation should bring in some innovative wins for everyone involved.

Does it improve the customer experience? If not, the innovative strategy must complement that ASAP before experiencing customer disengagement that leads to loss of the customer. What other value does the automation bring to the client? Faster process, not having to wait, gain in cost, gain in terms of options, flexibility, convenience? There are many more possibilities for innovation and delivering outstanding solutions.

Though the machine is supposed to support us humans, it is not always perceived as such and for good reasons. There is a gap between humans and computers, and that is also why we are complementary to each other. Every innovation should take into account the customer experience and mind the gap between the machine and the human (or animal) customer. Failing to do so may rip out the benefits of the investments in automation technology. This applies to artificial intelligence, automation, robotics, and all the like.

MEET AXEL FROM CORP 2

Solutions—Implementing transformation on the front side of customer experience.

Corp 2 specializes in the chartered vacation business. They deliver flights, hotels, and mobility services to their clients for some attractive vacation destinations. The international safety situation and economic crisis had caused them to lose a large part of their yearly revenue, and they were directly impacted by several bombings that took place around the world and restrain people's vacation desires.

Corp 2 was in a severe economic crisis. This led them to focus mainly on reducing their costs, since they had less revenue. They were replacing most of their people with machines in the form of online sales, online self-check-in, and onsite self-service check-in. There was no added value except for saving money for the company.

Soon, Corp 2 was confronted with another dilemma. On departure, the queue for the self-check-in gets longer and longer. People were frustrated with the machines, despite a couple of workers helping passengers. These clients were also going through more robust screening upon accessing the airports due to reinforced security related to the high terrorist alert that followed some terrible public bombings internationally.

The workers available were overwhelmed with their solicitation for processes on the machine that was not so smooth and friendly but as well because of additional compliance and security rules that were implemented in the system and that people were not familiar with.

Soon customers were sharing their experience on social media and describing how they have to face with new unknown regulations along with tightening remote security control and having in front of them, a machine that can't answer to their questions or assist them in such a delicate situation. Some even declare that their vacation starts badly and that they already dread the return.

On the other hand, there was other carriers who had implemented the self-check-in as well, but their story was entirely different for the customer experience. Soon, customers, who were already a few were going to the competitors after the bad press that the customer displays online and shared on social media. Corp 2 found itself in a situation where they were selling their packages below their break-even point to fill planes and hotels that were operating at below capacities. Worse than that, one of its competitors took on the complaints against Corp 2 and turned it into a funny, captivating, and damaging ad, to draw clients from Corp 2. The loss was more than they could take for long; therefore, they had to find a solution to turn things around profoundly. Their reputation was so damaged and the situation so dreadful that realigning with the market was not enough, they had to gain a competitive edge to be profitable again in a challenging context.

SORTING CORP 2 FROM THE DRAMATIC CRISIS

The first thing was to shift Corp 2 from the cost-saving mindset to an innovative transformation mindset. As a result of advised changes being quickly implemented, Corp 2 had:

1. Three separate options for checking in: online, onsite self-help with support, and human-assisted check-in.
2. With the right information and buy-in, they moved a large portion of their check in process online and the rest choose assisted check-in. The issue proved not to be with using machines but their failure to address the customer experience and the gap between the machine and the human.
3. The new business experience offered new and extended product range. New innovative solutions started attracting clients and redefining the customer experience.
4. Partnership with innovative clients who contributed to the business' transformation and improvement. In return, the clients were rewarded with additional exclusive advantages.
5. Winning partnerships in delivering innovative services to clients.
6. New revenue streams.
7. Improve customer experience and services.
8. Improved communication with clients and within Corp 2.

As a result, they were profitable and on track leading the market.

3. DIGITAL TRANSFORMATION TOOL CHAOS

Organizations experiencing digital tool chaos have acquired disparate tools without a focusing on the bigger picture or without properly researching the new tools to ensure they align with business strategy. Organizations that had experienced various tools, either because business units decided on tools separately, or again, that needed an additional tool at some point. Overlapping tools often reveal a misalignment in any of the following: between teams, business strategy, and/or technology strategy. Regardless of the cause, this is a situation where purchasing decisions were made without a clear vision of the strategic business vision. Often these misaligned decisions are based on fear, established relationships, and reliance on a vendor opinion.

Selecting and adopting new products can be a project on its own. It is important to research products, test them, and align them with your business strategy and vision before making a decision.

The process of selecting and adopting new technology products should satisfy the following steps:

1. Decide on the business needs—necessary features, mandatory outcomes, actual or future possibilities, integration needs, reporting needs, business data capabilities, budget, customization possibilities, option to use across the organization successfully.
2. Audit your tools to see if there are any existing tools that can meet the demands. Check to see if existing suppliers have additional solutions or upgrades that can be considered before looking elsewhere. (Only look to the vendor if the relationship is a positive one.)
3. List the tools on the market that can meet the business demand. Analyze other innovation capabilities and opportunities.

Rank based on product match and product future evolution or innovation strategy. Select at least five tools to investigate further and set up a trial.

4. Look at the businesses of these potential suppliers and their relationship potential for your company. Are they stable, funded? Do they continuously innovate? How often do they update their solutions? What about their service terms? Look at integration with other tools on the market, general customer experience, and reputation. Who is using their products? Has any great achievement come using their solutions? Rank suppliers by relationship desirability for your business.
5. Select the tools you want to try and contact them, test the products/services, validate against your previous criteria and final alignment with your business. This is best done organization-wide.

MEET DOMINIQUE FROM CORP 3

Dominique is an executive leader at a marketing and public relations firm that has been in business for about two decades and has a portfolio including some large clients in both the private and public sectors. Corp 3 has a year-round, full agenda, a team of about thirty people, and open collaboration with several suppliers.

Corp 3 overspent in communication, marketing, and social media tools. They had adopted a more contemporary approach of leading with technology. The approach is very common in business today because of social media and digital marketing technology innovations and offers exploding onto the market. Of the tools they invested in, some were not used, some rarely used, and many abandoned while still paying license fees for them.

They got to a point where delivery was slowed and the employees were blaming the tools for delays, integration failures, and poor service. Corp 3 depended mainly on multiple suppliers for support and solutions integration. Their IT specialist was overwhelmed and could not keep up.

To alleviate the situation, I had to help Dominique and Corp 3 leverage digital transformation in the following ways:

1. We reviewed their business strategy and updated it with their strategic vision.
2. Then I created the technology strategy to support their business strategy.
3. Then we went through the technology research and adoption process. We reviewed, analyzed, and measured all tools they had onboard and how they aligned with their tech strategy. We kept only the tools that aligned with their goals and complemented the new ones. We enlisted tool training, appreciation, performance measurement, and engagement testing. We initiated a specialist contract for integration and technical support with some of their suppliers.

As a result, production increased by 60 percent, and costs were reduced by 20 percent. Corp 3 experienced fewer bottlenecks and delayed deliveries.

4. COLLABORATIVE CHAOS

Collaborative chaos is the situation where businesses find themselves in conflict over progress, either within the company, with partners, or both. It is often a result of unclear or unsettled agreements about roles, responsibilities, and obligations.

Many partnerships are made quickly without describing the roles and responsibilities of every party. Also, it is often challenging to oversee all aspects of a relationship beforehand. Regardless, an authority must be established, and every party should be accountable for what relates to them, and at any time, try finding common ground and solutions for conflicts or challenges they face.

However, the world is not perfect and many collaborations lack the basic relationship definitions with goals or details about the objectives. Often one party may be in crisis and desperate for the other's help, and they neglect establishing written agreements, leaving their goals subjective. This is more common than we may think, especially with new technology.

Whatever the innovation, the technology, and the business understanding of the latest technology or concept, they should clarify what they want or, at least, how the solution from the other party will serve their business. If there is no in-house specialist who can lead the clarification part successfully (or even if they can), hire a neutral strategist or a specialist who can help the business to clarify what they want and how the partner can contribute to the business' success.

You want to adopt AI, hire an AI strategist to help before starting a relationship with any AI solution provider.

You want to implement business transformation, hire a digital transformation strategist to guide you before selecting technology and suppliers.

Remember that transformation happens with strategy first. You may have the best technology on hand and still fail if you have no plan or lack a transformative approach. Use your strategic plan to identify what you want, select the best suppliers, and specify your expectations from suppliers.

This is valid both for business solutions and terms of service, responsiveness, delivery, risk management, and change management. Your overall strategy can identify dependencies and additional collaboration, tools, and services you may need.

MEET SARAH FROM CORP 4

Sarah from Corp 4 was distressed about her organization's partnership with Company X. Agreements with Company X were:

1. Poorly drafted and/or non-existent.
2. Signed agreements lacked specific guidelines about delivery, services, and quality.
3. No renegotiation clause was included.
4. Stilted toward the supplier leaving Corp 4 at the mercy of the suppliers' goodwill.
5. Delivery delays and low quality threaten Corp 4's business reputation, delivery to its clients, and revenue.

Solution for Sarah and Corp 4:

1. Clarified business delivery expectations, service level agreement, and quality level.
2. Renegotiated what could be renegotiated and concluded new agreements, new work procedures, new contracts, additional investments, and timelines.
3. Addressed the cost of non-delivery: delays, penalty, rework, and changes.
4. Defined monitoring and measuring procedures.

As a result, business collaboration improved and productivity increased by 30 percent.

5. LOW LEVEL OF LEADERSHIP AND ACCOUNTABILITY

Meet John from Corp 5

John and Corp 5 struggling with poor project leadership and accountability. Several teams (internal and external) were working more or less independently toward a delivery. Team members exchange tasks like hot potatoes, while challenges were deep and severely tangled. The overall vision, directions, follow-up, and team support were poor. This led to poor team engagement. John was under pressure and used fear to force his team to deliver on time. All this led to constant blame games, lack of trust, and a cover your butt atmosphere where everyone focused on looking out for themselves.

SOLUTIONS FOR CORP 5, TO RECLAIM LEADERSHIP, ENGAGEMENT AND FACILITATE DELIVERY

1. Shift John's mindset from fear-based management and leadership. Then shift the team's mindset.
2. Help John create and communicate a detailed description of project scope, vision, direction, and goals.
3. Review team members' roles and relevancies.
4. Help John lead by example and inspire his team (accountability, ownership, improved communication, and effective coordination) and gain their trust.
5. Create team spirit through workshops, problem-solving, and learning to win together.
6. Develop work procedures, communication procedures, and standardized tools.
7. Create timelines for goals, schedule rewards, lessons learned sessions, and celebrations.

SUMMARY

Let's wrap this chapter up by looking at the top nine facts about digital transformation today:

1. The success of digital transformation depends on the strategy first, not the technology.
2. It is essential to have an aligned digital transformation leadership team for rapid and sustainable transformation implementation.
3. Any organization that focuses on automatization instead of innovation may soon be left behind or become outdated.
4. Most technology programs or systems for transformation are new and untested.
5. These tools, though targeted, are made for a broad audience and not with one in particular organization in mind.
6. People who are paid to sell a solution always claim it is the best and can solve your issues.
7. There are too few great leaders with a transformative vision.
8. Most organizations underestimate the need to invest in individual transformation first.
9. Transformation is a continuous learning journey.

CHAPTER 16

Embracing Artificial Intelligence: The New Frontier for Business

Artificial Intelligence (AI) in 2025 – 2026 is no longer a futuristic concept limited to science fiction or niche tech companies. It is a powerful and transformative force reshaping every facet of business across industries worldwide. For companies seeking to maintain competitive advantage, increase efficiency, and innovate rapidly, understanding and adopting AI technologies is no longer optional, it is imperative.

This chapter explores the broad landscape of AI technologies today, categorizing key types, their uses, and practical applications. We will delve into how automation powered by AI is revolutionizing workflows, examine breakthrough inventions such as self-driving cars, and explore the technological backbone propelling these advances, including supercomputing and cloud infrastructure.

UNDERSTANDING THE CATEGORIES AND SUBCATEGORIES OF ARTIFICIAL INTELLIGENCE (AI)

AI is an umbrella term that covers a vast array of technologies and methodologies. While definitions vary, we can group AI into several broad categories, each with distinct capabilities and business use cases:

1. Machine Learning (ML)

Machine Learning is the foundation of most AI applications today. It enables computers to learn from data without explicit programming. ML algorithms identify patterns, make predictions, and improve through experience.

- **Supervised Learning:** Uses labeled data to train models for classification or regression tasks (e.g., fraud detection, customer churn prediction).
- **Unsupervised Learning:** Finds hidden patterns in unlabeled data (e.g., customer segmentation, anomaly detection).
- **Reinforcement Learning:** Models learn optimal actions via trial and error with feedback (used in robotics, game playing, and autonomous systems).

Business uses: Personalized marketing, risk assessment, predictive maintenance, demand forecasting, credit scoring.

2. Natural Language Processing (NLP)

NLP focuses on enabling machines to understand, interpret, and generate human language. It bridges the gap between humans and machines, allowing more natural interactions.

- **Sentiment Analysis:** Understanding customer opinions in text data (social media, reviews).

- **Chatbots and Virtual Assistants:** Automated customer service and support.
- **Language Translation:** Real-time and automated language conversion.
- **Text Summarization and Document Classification:** Extracting key information and categorizing documents.

Business uses: Customer service automation, brand reputation monitoring, document processing, multilingual communication.

3. Generative AI

Generative AI refers to systems capable of creating new content, text, images, music, or even code - often indistinguishable from human-created works.

- **Generative Adversarial Networks (GANs):** Used to generate realistic images or video.
- **Transformer Models (e.g., GPT, BERT):** Power advanced language models for text generation and understanding.

Business uses: Content creation, marketing copy, product design prototyping, virtual environments, coding assistants.

4. Robotics and Autonomous Systems

Robotics integrates AI with mechanical systems to automate physical tasks. Autonomous systems include robots, drones, and self-driving vehicles that operate with minimal human input.

- **Industrial Robots:** Automating manufacturing processes such as assembly and packaging.
- **Service Robots:** Delivery robots, cleaning bots, customer-facing robots.

- **Autonomous Vehicles:** Self-driving cars, trucks, drones for logistics and transport.

Business uses: Manufacturing efficiency, last-mile delivery, warehouse automation, transportation logistics.

5. Agentic AI

Agentic AI refers to AI systems capable of autonomous decision-making, planning, and task execution—often called AI agents. These systems can operate independently, sometimes chaining multiple tasks without human intervention.

- **Intelligent Personal Assistants:** Beyond simple commands, these agents handle complex workflows.
- **Automated Process Management:** Managing business processes end-to-end with minimal oversight.
- **Multi-agent Systems:** Collaborative AI entities working together for complex goals.

Business uses: Workflow automation, IT service management, complex customer interactions, supply chain coordination.

6. Computer Vision

Computer vision allows machines to interpret and analyze visual data from the world, including images and videos.

- **Image Recognition:** Identifying objects, people, or text in images.
- **Facial Recognition:** Authentication and security.
- **Quality Inspection:** Automated defect detection in manufacturing.

Business uses: Security surveillance, retail checkout automation, medical imaging, autonomous vehicles.

AUTOMATION: THE PURPOSE AND IMPACT ON BUSINESS

At the core of AI adoption in business lies **automation**—the ability to perform repetitive, rule-based, or even complex tasks without human intervention. Automation powered by AI goes beyond traditional scripted automation by learning from data and adapting to new conditions.

The benefits of automation include:

- **Increased efficiency and speed:** Machines work 24/7 without fatigue.
- **Improved accuracy and consistency:** Reducing human error.
- **Cost reduction:** Lower labor costs and optimized resource use.
- **Scalability:** Rapid scaling of operations without proportional human resource increases.
- **Enhanced customer experience:** Faster response times and personalized services.

For example, AI-driven chatbots handle millions of customer queries simultaneously, freeing human agents to focus on complex issues. Predictive maintenance in manufacturing reduces downtime by forecasting failures before they occur.

TRANSFORMATIONAL AI-POWERED INNOVATIONS RESHAPING BUSINESS

Artificial intelligence is no longer confined to algorithms running in the background; it powers groundbreaking inventions changing entire industries and business models.

SELF-DRIVING VEHICLES AND AUTONOMOUS SYSTEMS

One of the most visible AI breakthroughs is **autonomous vehicles** self-driving cars, trucks, drones, and ships—that promise to revolutionize transportation and logistics.

- **Self-Driving Cars:** Companies like Tesla, Waymo, and others have developed cars capable of navigating urban environments with minimal human intervention. These vehicles utilize a combination of computer vision, sensor fusion, and reinforcement learning to make split-second driving decisions.
- **Autonomous Trucks:** Long-haul freight is a key target, with companies deploying autonomous trucks to reduce driver shortages and increase efficiency on highways.
- **Drones and Delivery Robots:** Drones are increasingly used for rapid delivery in urban and remote areas, transforming last-mile logistics.
- **Maritime and Aviation:** Autonomous ships and aircraft are in development to enhance safety and efficiency in sea and air freight.

Business impact: Autonomous systems reduce labor costs, increase safety, and enable new services. They disrupt insurance, urban planning, retail delivery, and supply chain models.

SUPERCOMPUTING AND CLOUD INFRASTRUCTURE POWERING AI

Behind AI's rapid progress is a powerful technological backbone—**supercomputers** and cloud computing infrastructure enabling massive data processing and training of complex AI models.

- **Supercomputers:** High-performance computing clusters with thousands of GPUs process massive datasets and train advanced models like GPT-4 or large-scale vision systems.
- **Cloud Computing:** Platforms like AWS, Azure, and Google Cloud provide scalable, on-demand resources allowing businesses of all sizes to deploy AI solutions without heavy upfront investment.
- **Edge Computing:** Processing data close to its source (e.g., IoT devices) reduces latency and supports real-time AI applications in manufacturing, autonomous vehicles, and healthcare.

Business impact: Democratizes access to AI technology, accelerates innovation cycles, and supports new data-driven business models.

PRACTICAL CONSIDERATIONS FOR AI ADOPTION IN BUSINESS

Implementing AI is not just about technology, successful adoption requires strategic alignment, ethical considerations, change management, and digital leadership.

IDENTIFYING BUSINESS USE CASES

Not every AI tool fits every business. Leaders should start by identifying pain points and opportunities where AI can add measurable value. Examples include:

- Customer service automation with chatbots (NLP).
- Fraud detection and risk management (ML).
- Predictive maintenance and supply chain optimization (ML, IoT).

- Personalized marketing campaigns (generative AI).
- Automated content creation for social media and advertising (generative AI).

INTEGRATION WITH EXISTING SYSTEMS

AI must often work alongside legacy systems. Planning seamless integration, data flow, and interoperability is critical to avoid silos and maximize ROI.

DATA STRATEGY AND GOVERNANCE

AI thrives on data, so businesses must develop robust data strategies—ensuring quality, privacy, and compliance with regulations like GDPR.

TALENT AND CULTURE

AI adoption demands new skills: data scientists, AI specialists, and cross-functional teams who understand both technology and business processes. Cultural readiness and leadership support are essential.

ETHICAL AND RESPONSIBLE AI

Businesses must commit to transparency, fairness, and mitigating bias in AI models to maintain trust and comply with evolving regulations.

THE ROAD AHEAD

The AI landscape is evolving rapidly. Emerging trends include:

- **Agentic AI and Autonomous Agents:** AI systems capable of complex decision-making and managing workflows end-to-end.
- **Explainable AI:** Improving transparency to make AI decisions understandable and auditable.
- **AI Democratization:** Tools enabling non-experts to build and deploy AI solutions.
- **Human-AI Collaboration:** Designing systems where AI augments human work rather than replaces it.

AI ADOPTION ACROSS KEY INDUSTRIES

Artificial intelligence is transforming every sector, but its adoption and impact vary based on industry-specific challenges and opportunities. Below are some of the most significant sectors embracing AI today.

HEALTHCARE

AI is revolutionizing healthcare by enabling faster diagnosis, personalized treatment, and improved patient outcomes.

- **Medical Imaging and Diagnostics:** AI-powered computer vision systems analyze X-rays, MRIs, and pathology slides to detect anomalies faster and more accurately than human experts.

- **Predictive Analytics:** Machine learning models predict patient deterioration, hospital readmissions, and disease outbreaks.
- **Drug Discovery:** Generative AI accelerates drug molecule design, reducing development time and costs.
- **Virtual Health Assistants:** NLP-based chatbots support patient triage, appointment scheduling, and medication adherence.

Impact: Improved quality of care, reduced costs, and expanded access to medical services.

FINANCE

AI helps financial institutions manage risk, personalize services, and fight fraud.

- **Fraud Detection:** Machine learning models detect suspicious transactions in real-time.
- **Algorithmic Trading:** AI analyzes vast data to execute trades at high speeds and optimized timing.
- **Credit Scoring:** Alternative data and ML models improve lending decisions and inclusion.
- **Customer Service:** Chatbots handle routine inquiries, freeing human agents for complex tasks.

Impact: Enhanced security, operational efficiency, and customer experience.

RETAIL AND E-COMMERCE

Retailers leverage AI to create personalized experiences, optimize inventory, and improve supply chains.

- **Recommendation Engines:** AI suggests products based on user behavior and preferences.
- **Inventory Forecasting:** ML predicts demand to reduce stock-outs and overstock.
- **Visual Search:** Computer vision lets customers search by image rather than text.
- **Automated Checkout:** Robotics and AI-powered self-checkout improve speed and reduce labor.

Impact: Increased sales, reduced waste, and elevated customer satisfaction.

MANUFACTURING AND SUPPLY CHAIN

AI enhances production efficiency, quality control, and logistics management.

- **Predictive Maintenance:** Sensors and ML predict equipment failures before they occur.
- **Quality Inspection:** Computer vision automates defect detection on assembly lines.
- **Supply Chain Optimization:** AI forecasts demand, manages inventory, and routes shipments.
- **Robotics:** Collaborative robots (cobots) work alongside humans for flexibility.

Impact: Reduced downtime, higher product quality, and optimized operations.

GOVERNANCE AND LEADERSHIP IMPERATIVES FOR AI SUCCESS

Adopting AI responsibly and effectively demands more than technology, it requires a commitment to governance and enlightened leadership.

ESTABLISHING AN AI STRATEGY

Leaders must develop a clear vision aligned with business goals. This includes prioritizing AI projects that deliver tangible value and planning for long-term scalability.

ETHICAL AI AND COMPLIANCE

AI systems must be designed and monitored to avoid biases, ensure fairness, and protect privacy. Transparent communication with stakeholders about AI use builds trust.

BUILDING AI COMPETENCY

Investing in talent development and cross-functional teams that blend domain expertise with AI skills is critical. Leaders should foster a culture of continuous learning and experimentation.

CHANGE MANAGEMENT AND COMMUNICATION

Successful AI adoption hinges on preparing employees for new ways of working. Leaders must communicate the purpose of AI, address fears about job disruption, and involve teams in co-creating AI solutions.

MEASURING IMPACT AND ACCOUNTABILITY

Clear metrics and KPIs should track AI performance and business outcomes. Governance structures must assign accountability for AI systems and their decisions.

The opportunities are wide and deep. We need innovative leaders to leverage the true power of artificial intelligence not just once through automation, but on a continuous basis. A great hint? Look for problems and conflict to either solve or develop new experience for.

CHAPTER 17

Leading Job Reinvention: Building Digitally Intelligent Human-Machine Teams

REAL-WORLD EXAMPLES OF FEAR IN AI ADOPTION

EMPLOYEE EXAMPLE: AMAZON WAREHOUSE AUTOMATION

Amazon's increasing use of robots in warehouses has boosted efficiency but also stirred anxiety among workers about job security. Reports have shown some employees fearing replacement or being pushed into physically demanding roles. Amazon has responded with retraining programs and role shifts to balance automation with workforce empowerment.

CUSTOMER EXAMPLE: CHATBOT FRUSTRATION IN BANKING

Banks implementing AI chatbots to handle customer inquiries often face frustration when chatbots fail to understand complex issues. Customers fear losing personal service, prompting banks to implement "human-in-the-loop" systems where humans step in seamlessly when needed.

ORGANIZATIONAL EXAMPLE: AI SURVEILLANCE AT WORK

Some companies use AI-powered monitoring to track employee productivity, raising privacy concerns and fear of micromanagement. Transparent policies, opt-in programs, and focusing on empowering employees rather than penalizing them help alleviate fears.

CONVERTING FEAR INTO MOTIVATION FOR INNOVATION

Managing these fears proactively is not just about mitigation, it's an opportunity to ignite **innovation and creativity** that strengthens organizational resilience and customer loyalty.

STRATEGIES FOR EMPLOYEE ENGAGEMENT AND EMPOWERMENT

- **Transparent Communication:** Share openly about AI goals, timelines, and impacts. Address fears directly with facts and empathy.
- **Inclusive Co-Creation:** Involve employees in AI design and deployment decisions to build ownership and reduce resistance.
- **Continuous Learning Culture:** Offer accessible training programs and career pathway planning aligned with new AI-augmented roles.

- **Human-AI Collaboration Messaging:** Frame AI as a tool to amplify human skills, not replace them. Showcase success stories of employees leveraging AI to do more meaningful work.
- **Wellbeing Focus:** Recognize change fatigue and provide mental health support, flexible work options, and spaces for open dialogue.

STRATEGIES FOR ENHANCING CUSTOMER EXPERIENCE

- **Hybrid Service Models:** Blend AI efficiency with human empathy by enabling smooth transitions between chatbots and live agents.
- **Transparent Data Use:** Clearly explain data policies and give customers control over their information.
- **Ethical AI Practices:** Commit publicly to fair, bias-free AI and include customers in feedback loops to build trust.
- **Personalization and Usability:** Use AI to customize experiences without overwhelming or confusing users. Simplify interfaces and keep human help accessible.
- **Demonstrate Value:** Communicate how AI enhances service speed, accuracy, and convenience.

INSPIRATIONAL EXAMPLES OF INNOVATION FUELED BY MANAGING FEAR

MICROSOFT'S AI UPSKILLING INITIATIVE

Microsoft launched an ambitious program to retrain over 25 million people worldwide for the AI economy, emphasizing that new skills empower workers rather than displace them. Their messaging centers on AI augmenting human potential, inspiring employees and partners to embrace change.

SEPHORA'S AI-POWERED PERSONALIZED BEAUTY

Sephora uses AI-driven virtual try-ons and personalized recommendations to enhance customer experience. They combine AI with expert human consultants, addressing fears of impersonal service and fostering innovation in retail.

MAYO CLINIC'S AI FOR PATIENT CARE

Mayo Clinic integrates AI diagnostics alongside physician expertise. Patients are informed of AI's role in their care, ensuring trust and acceptance. Staff are trained to use AI tools as assistants, promoting a culture of human-AI collaboration.

CREATING A CULTURE WHERE FEAR BECOMES FUEL

For leaders, the ultimate challenge is cultivating an environment where **fear is acknowledged but does not paralyze action**—where it becomes a catalyst for creative problem-solving and continuous innovation. This requires:

- **Empathy-Driven Leadership:** Listening actively, validating concerns, and communicating hope and vision.
- **Experimentation and Safe Failure:** Encouraging teams to test new AI applications without fear of punishment if they stumble.

- **Recognition and Celebration:** Highlighting stories of individuals and teams who turn fear into breakthroughs.
- **Building Trust Through Consistency:** Following through on promises, maintaining transparency, and prioritizing ethical AI use.

THE PEOPLE-CENTERED AI REVOLUTION

AI adoption is as much a people journey as it is a technological one. By understanding and addressing the fears of employees and customers, organizations can unlock **new levels of engagement, creativity, and loyalty**.

Transforming fear into motivation creates a powerful virtuous cycle—one where innovation flourishes, digital transformation succeeds, and people feel valued and empowered in the AI-driven future.

THE LEADER'S ROLE IN JOB REINVENTION AMID AI DISRUPTION

Exploring how AI is changing work, the imperative to retrain and upskill employees, and the vision for digitally intelligent teams where humans and machines collaborate effectively. I'll include sector examples and emerging roles.

As artificial intelligence accelerates transformation across industries, one of the most critical leadership challenges is **job reinvention**. AI is reshaping not just tasks but entire roles and career paths, demanding a proactive response from leaders to reimagine work, reskill employees, and foster seamless collaboration between humans and intelligent machines.

This chapter explores the leader's pivotal role in guiding organizations through this reinvention, building digitally intelligent teams where humans and AI co-create value, innovate continuously, and compete in the new economy.

> ***They say AI will create more jobs that it eliminates. I say, "AI won't create jobs. Leaders are creating jobs in the age of AI."***
> ***M. Nadia Vincent***

THE IMPERATIVE FOR JOB REINVENTION IN THE AGE OF AI

AI automates routine, repetitive tasks at unprecedented speed and scale, transforming workflows and operational models. However, rather than simply eliminating jobs, AI creates opportunities to redefine work, elevate human contributions, and unlock new roles focused on creativity, judgment, and complex problem-solving.

Leaders must:

- Anticipate which roles will evolve and which new roles will emerge.
- Prepare employees to transition from task execution to strategic, analytical, and interpersonal functions.
- Foster a culture that embraces lifelong learning and agility.

THE LEADER'S ROLE: CHAMPIONING JOB REINVENTION

1. VISIONARY WORKFORCE PLANNING

Leaders should use AI-driven analytics combined with human insight to forecast workforce needs. This includes:

- Mapping current roles against emerging AI capabilities.
- Identifying skill gaps and future skill requirements.
- Designing career pathways aligned with evolving organizational priorities.

2. COMPREHENSIVE RESKILLING AND UPSKILLING

Job reinvention requires broad learning initiatives:

- **AI Literacy for All:** Basic understanding of AI's capabilities, limitations, and ethical considerations for every employee.
- **Role-Specific Training:** Tailored programs teaching employees how to use AI tools relevant to their tasks.
- **Soft Skills Development:** Emphasis on creativity, emotional intelligence, critical thinking, and collaboration—skills that complement AI.

3. CULTIVATING HUMAN-AI COLLABORATION MINDSET

Leadership should foster a mindset that views AI as an augmentation partner, not a threat:

- Encourage employees to experiment with AI tools.
- Highlight examples of successful human-AI teamwork.
- Promote transparency about AI decision-making to build trust.

BUILDING THE DIGITALLY INTELLIGENT TEAM: ROLES FOR HUMANS AND AI

In digitally intelligent teams, humans and AI systems play complementary roles that maximize strengths. Consider these patterns:

- **AI as Data Analyst and Automator:** AI excels at processing large datasets, detecting patterns, automating repetitive tasks, and generating predictive insights.
- **Humans as Strategists and Empaths:** Humans bring contextual understanding, ethical judgment, creativity, and interpersonal skills necessary for complex decisions and relationship management.
- **Agentic AI and Autonomous Systems:** Emerging AI agents can perform sequences of tasks independently, enabling humans to focus on oversight and exception management.

SECTOR EXAMPLES OF JOB REINVENTION WITH AI

HEALTHCARE: FROM DATA ENTRY TO CARE COORDINATION

- **Before AI:** Nurses and administrative staff spent significant time on paperwork and manual data entry.
- **With AI:** Automation reduces paperwork, while AI analytics support clinical decisions. Nurses evolve into care coordinators who interpret AI insights, provide empathetic patient care, and manage complex cases.
- **New Roles:** AI specialists embedded in clinical teams, patient data ethicists, telehealth coordinators leveraging AI-enabled diagnostics.

FINANCE: FROM TRANSACTION PROCESSING TO RISK STRATEGY

- **Before AI:** Many analysts manually processed transactions and compliance reports.
- **With AI:** Robotic process automation (RPA) handles transaction processing and compliance checks. Analysts focus on risk strategy, model validation, and client advisory services.

- **New Roles:** AI governance officers, explainability experts ensuring transparent AI decisions, hybrid financial advisors using AI insights.

MANUFACTURING: FROM ASSEMBLY LINE TO ROBOTICS SUPERVISOR

- **Before AI:** Operators performed repetitive assembly tasks.
- **With AI:** Collaborative robots (cobots) work alongside humans, performing precision tasks. Operators transition to robotics supervisors, managing robot fleets and maintaining systems.
- **New Roles:** Robotics trainers, AI maintenance technicians, data analysts optimizing production using AI-generated insights.

RETAIL: FROM CASHIERS TO CUSTOMER EXPERIENCE DESIGNERS

- **Before AI:** Cashiers managed checkouts and inventory manually.
- **With AI:** Automated checkout systems reduce cashier roles. Employees shift to personalized customer experience design, using AI-generated customer insights to curate offerings.
- **New Roles:** AI customer experience strategists, virtual shopping assistants, omnichannel marketing analysts.

TRAINING EMPLOYEES TO WORK EFFECTIVELY WITH AI

Effective training programs combine:

- **Hands-On Experience:** Simulations and real projects using AI tools in employees' daily workflows.
- **Continuous Learning:** Microlearning, online courses, and peer learning to keep pace with rapid AI evolution.
- **Interdisciplinary Approach:** Blending technical AI knowledge with domain-specific expertise.
- **Emotional and Ethical Awareness:** Understanding AI's societal impacts and fostering responsible use.

LEADERSHIP ACTIONS TO DRIVE JOB REINVENTION

- **Communicate a Compelling Vision:** Help employees see AI as an enabler of more meaningful work.
- **Provide Psychological Safety:** Encourage experimentation and learning without fear of failure.
- **Invest in Partnerships:** Collaborate with educational institutions and AI vendors to access up-to-date training resources.
- **Monitor and Adapt:** Use data-driven insights to track progress and adjust workforce strategies.

SOME CASE STUDIES

CASE STUDIES: TRANSFORMING FEAR INTO INNOVATION

CASE STUDY 1: IBM WATSON'S JOURNEY IN HEALTHCARE AI

IBM's Watson AI platform promised revolutionary breakthroughs in healthcare diagnostics and treatment recommendations. However, early deployments faced skepticism from clinicians concerned about AI accuracy and job displacement.

How IBM addressed the fears:

- **Collaborative Development:** IBM involved doctors and medical staff early in system design and testing, making them co-creators rather than passive users.
- **Transparency and Education:** Extensive training programs clarified AI's role as a support tool—not a replacement—and showcased cases where AI enhanced clinical decisions.
- **Human-in-the-Loop Models:** Emphasized that final decisions rest with medical professionals, preserving human judgment.

Outcome: Over time, trust grew, and many institutions successfully integrated Watson into workflows, improving diagnostic speed and accuracy while maintaining clinician confidence.

CASE STUDY 2: DOMINO'S PIZZA – AI-POWERED CUSTOMER EXPERIENCE

Domino's introduced AI-powered ordering through chatbots and voice assistants, raising customer concerns about losing personal interaction and making mistakes with orders.

How Domino's managed customer fears:

- **Hybrid Model:** Allowed customers to switch to human agents anytime during the interaction.
- **Clear Communication:** Marketing and app interfaces

explained how AI simplified ordering while humans remained available.

- **Continuous Improvement:** Collected and acted on customer feedback to refine chatbot understanding and responsiveness.

Outcome: Customer satisfaction improved, order errors decreased, and Domino's reported increased online sales, with many customers appreciating the convenience of AI-enhanced service.

CASE STUDY 3: UNILEVER'S WORKFORCE UPSKILLING AMID AI INTEGRATION

Unilever introduced AI in manufacturing and supply chain, triggering employee anxiety about job security and skill relevance.

How Unilever converted fear into motivation:

- **Transparent Dialogues:** Leadership held town halls to discuss AI's impact honestly and outline reskilling plans.
- **Personalized Training:** Offered tailored upskilling programs to help workers transition into higher-value roles, such as AI monitoring and maintenance.
- **Recognition Programs:** Celebrated employees who embraced new skills and contributed innovative ideas for AI use.

Outcome: Employee engagement increased, turnover decreased, and Unilever reported productivity gains with a more digitally fluent workforce.

PRACTICAL EXERCISES FOR LEADERS TO MANAGE FEAR AND INSPIRE INNOVATION

Exercise 1: Fear Mapping Workshop

Objective: Identify and understand specific fears related to AI adoption within your organization.

Steps:

1. Gather cross-functional teams in small groups.
2. Ask participants to list fears they associate with AI adoption—for themselves, their teams, and customers.
3. Group similar fears and discuss root causes.
4. Prioritize the top 3 fears that need immediate attention.
5. Brainstorm strategies to address these fears—through communication, training, policy changes, or process redesign.
6. Assign owners and timelines for follow-up actions.

Outcome: Creates a shared awareness of fears and a proactive plan to address them, fostering trust and engagement.

Exercise 2: Human-AI Collaboration Role Play

Objective: Help employees visualize and experience AI as a supportive partner rather than a threat.

Steps:

1. Design scenarios where employees use AI tools in daily tasks (e.g., customer service chatbot assisting human agents).
2. Divide participants into pairs or small groups playing roles—human worker, AI assistant, and customer.
3. Act out the scenario, focusing on how AI complements human skills.
4. Debrief to discuss feelings, insights, and potential improvements.

Outcome: Reduces anxiety by demonstrating practical AI collaboration and highlighting the value humans bring.

Exercise 3: Customer Empathy Mapping for AI Experiences
Objective: Understand customer emotions and expectations regarding AI interactions to design better experiences.

Steps:

1. Create empathy maps capturing what customers say, think, feel, and do when interacting with AI-powered services.
2. Identify pain points and moments of delight.
3. Brainstorm design principles and service adjustments that address fears and enhance trust.
4. Develop simple prototypes or communication messages to test with real customers.

Outcome: Customer-centric AI designs that reduce fears and improve satisfaction and loyalty.

Exercise 4: Innovation Challenge: Turning Fear into Opportunity
Objective: Empower teams to propose innovative solutions addressing AI-related fears or barriers.

Steps:

1. Organize a time-bound challenge inviting teams to identify a specific fear or challenge related to AI adoption.
2. Encourage creative solutions, process changes, new tools, communication campaigns, training modules, etc.
3. Provide resources and leadership support for prototyping.
4. Showcase and reward promising ideas.

Outcome: Engages employees in positive problem-solving, strengthens ownership, and surfaces actionable innovations.

IN CONCLUSION, LEADING THE PEOPLE-CENTERED AI TRANSFORMATION

Leaders who acknowledge and address the emotional and experiential aspects of AI adoption build stronger, more agile organizations. By turning fear into a catalyst for innovation, they create environments where employees and customers feel heard, valued, and motivated to co-create the future.

Managing the people's experience is not a one-time effort but an ongoing commitment, one that will differentiate successful AI transformations in the years to come.

Job reinvention is not a threat but a transformative opportunity, one that demands visionary leadership, investment in people, and a culture that embraces change. By building digitally intelligent teams where humans and AI work in harmony, leaders can unlock unprecedented innovation, resilience, and growth in the evolving digital economy.

SOME TOOLS

1. WORKFORCE AI READINESS ASSESSMENT FRAMEWORK

Purpose: Evaluate how prepared your workforce is to adopt and work effectively alongside AI, identifying gaps and strengths.

Dimension	Key Questions	Assessment Criteria	Action Focus
AI Awareness	Do employees understand AI basics and potential?	% of employees with basic AI literacy training	Provide foundational AI education
Skill Alignment	Are current skills aligned with AI-augmented roles?	Skills inventory vs future role requirements	Develop targeted upskilling/reskilling programs
Change Mindset	Are employees open to change and new ways of working?	Survey results on attitudes toward AI and innovation	Change management and culture building
Access to Tools	Do employees have access and training on AI tools?	Availability of AI software/tools and usage rates	Invest in user-friendly AI tools and training
Leadership Support	Are leaders visibly supporting AI adoption?	Leadership communications, resources dedicated to AI adoption	Leadership development and communication plans

Usage: Conduct surveys, interviews, and skills audits mapped against this framework to get a holistic readiness score and identify gaps.

2. JOB REINVENTION AND RESKILLING PLANNING FRAMEWORK

Purpose: Guide leaders through mapping, redesigning, and reskilling jobs affected by AI.

Step	Description	Deliverables
Role Mapping	Identify roles impacted by AI (e.g., automated, augmented, new roles)	Role impact matrix
Skill Gap Analysis	Assess current skills vs future skills needed	Skill gap reports
Role Redesign	Define new role descriptions integrating AI collaboration	Updated job descriptions
Training Program Design	Develop learning paths for upskilling/ reskilling	Curriculum outlines, learning modules
Pilot and Feedback	Run pilot training, gather feedback, and iterate	Pilot reports, improvement plans
Full Rollout & Support	Implement full program with ongoing support	Training schedules, coaching plans

3. AI TRAINING PROGRAM DESIGN FRAMEWORK

Purpose: Structure effective AI training for employees to build confidence and competence.

Component	Key Elements	Examples
Foundation	AI literacy: basics of AI, ethics, impact	Online courses, webinars, AI 101 workshops
Role-Specific Skills	Hands-on use of AI tools relevant to job functions	CRM AI features for sales, predictive analytics for finance, AI diagnostics for healthcare workers
Soft Skills	Creativity, critical thinking, collaboration, adaptability	Workshops, role-playing, group projects
Human-AI Collaboration	Understanding AI as a partner, transparency, trust-building	Case studies, simulation exercises
Continuous Learning	Microlearning, AI updates, peer communities	Learning platforms, newsletters, AI user groups

BONUS: SAMPLE AI READINESS SELF-ASSESSMENT SURVEY ITEMS

- I understand how AI tools will impact my daily work.
- I feel confident using AI applications relevant to my role.
- I am willing to learn new skills to work effectively with AI.
- I trust the leadership to support us through AI-driven changes.
- I believe AI will help me perform better, not replace me.

A FINAL NOTE

"Life's most persistent and urgent question is, 'What are you doing for others?"

- MARTIN LUTHER KING, JR

Leading digital transformation is unlike project management in that it does not have an end. It is a circular process where, after you close an iteration, you continue, just with more experience, and hopefully, lessons learned you can capitalize on. The digital transformation leader is like a scout, always prepared. If you have been a scout, you know what I mean. Whatever the situation, you must make the best of it, working with what you have.

The digital transformation leader can also be seen as a "MacGyver," the character played by Richard Dean Anderson on the television series by the same name that ran from 1985 to 1992 (and was reprised by Lucas Till in 2016). They must be creative, innovative, and resourceful! MacGyver never used a gun. Non-violent, he intelligently uses everyday objects as tools to overcome even the most hopeless situation with perseverance, creativity, and the determination to do good.

For you as a digital leader, the great news is that the tools available to you today are "smart." Therefore, many tasks you used to do yourself or that your team did before may be automated or delegated. Remember to not feel useless when some of your skills are not needed anymore but to accept and grow toward your next assignment.

I have shown you how your brain is the most powerful computer that exist and that you can upgrade the software running in it to achieve more by transforming yourself. Think above the smart tools that you have on hand and innovate something greater for you, your business, your industry, and for the good of our planet.

The digital transformation formula will work for you as long as you remember to integrate each value of the equation. Though it is a universal formula, personalize it with your own individual flavor suitable for your business or organization. That is the secret to innovation.

Innovation will shape our future, and I encourage every transformation leader to dedicate at least 10 percent of their energy to that. Our world will not just happen but will become as we innovate it to be.

Today's technologies will be different than tomorrow's as our vision and goals evolve. We should remember to not be too dependent on or even attached to the technology but to use it as one of our tools without ever neglecting the unmatched human brain and the business strategy.

Business has always been an exchange since the beginning but the way we do business, our strategies, change over time. Our children will most likely do business differently than we do but a business strategy will always prevail. As for today, always have a digital business strategy. Your digital business strategy should cover more than just your digital tools. Remember to incorporate all the values in the formula, such as the individual, the business, the technology, and every interaction between these where fear can be an obstacle to achieving your goals or vision.

Your vision should be clear, transformative, shared, and supported.

Refrain from having your vision in your head only. That leads to confusion, misalignment, and loss of trust from your team or stakeholders. The progress toward your vision and goals will be better monitored or tracked on paper, not in your head. And if you don't have your vision clear and on paper, it is more challenging to create motivated missionaries who will help create the vision. Sharing is caring for your vision. Unless if it is not a positive one, then sooner or later you will encounter disengagement.

A disengaged organization is one of the most costly to run. In such an environment, negative energy thrives, and we know that emotions are contagious. You can deduce that from the illustration of how the brain works in Chapter 3. You don't want to focus on negative energy and allow it to breed in your organization. Focus on positive energy, on your goals, your vision, and guide your team or your organization to do so as well. Lead by example.

Your people are watching you, how you lead, how you engage, the energy you bring into the organization, how you handle both failure and success, your performance level, and the performance level you expect from them. Define the rules, live the values, inspire and enforce participation, define rewards and responsibilities. Don't expect an easy ride but make it exciting. Together with your people, create an awesome culture that promotes individual transformation, flexibility, well-being, performance, innovation, effectiveness, business success, and happiness. That's the true reflection of the digitally transformed environment.

Finally, I invite you to join my online community of digital transformation leaders at digitaltransformationleaders.com. I've created the platform with the intention to guide more leaders. You will find articles, coaching programs, webinars, training, innovation news, events, and more. You can contribute to the transformation of other leaders by posting articles, descriptions of innovations and tools, and lessons learned. There are also several coaching and training programs you can follow online, either in real time or self-paced. It is a great place to learn about ongoing events worldwide focused on leadership and digital transformation.

Follow me on my social media accounts for regular updates.
Twitter: @ITTransleaders
LinkedIn: M. Nadia Vincent
Thank you for choosing this book.
Best wishes!
Nadia

BONUS SECTION

The Ultimate Executive Guide for Embracing Artificial Intelligence

WHAT IS ARTIFICIAL INTELLIGENCE?

You may search and find multiple definitions of artificial intelligence, but in this guide, I'll define artificial intelligence as the intelligence provided by machines or computers. Artificial intelligence is different from our gifted human intelligence. However, artificial intelligence is created by us, humans; we use our human intelligence as models for artificial intelligence and build it to support human intelligence. As a result, we can do additional things we could not do easily with our limited human capacity, but that we can empower a machine, computer, or robot to do.

Inside our human intelligence, we have many capabilities or many types of intelligence. For example, our multiple intelligences relate to speaking ability, calculating ability, sensorial ability, analytics capability, emotional capabilities, etc. In artificial intelligence, just like in human intelligence, many types of intelligence also exist. We refer to them in different terms such as natural language processing, robotics, machine learning, deep learning, neural networks, and cognitive computing, beyond others.

Artificial intelligence does not exist by itself for we humans fabricate it, and therefore, it uses the intelligence that relates to our natural human abilities. However, though artificial intelligence refers to our human intelligence, it cannot replace our human intelligence. Not now at least, as backed up by all the research carried out at the pioneer and world-renowned MIT laboratories over the last fifty-plus years, and also the countless business implementations of artificial intelligence happening worldwide.

Artificial intelligence can support human intelligence in numerous ways; it can perform tasks that would have been impossible for our human intelligence to do in record time. Artificial intelligence challenges our human intelligence to think higher and delegate the routine and the menial tasks to machines.

REAL ARTIFICIAL INTELLIGENCE VS. SCIENCE-FICTION ARTIFICIAL INTELLIGENCE

Real artificial intelligence today is different from science-fiction artificial intelligence that we see in the movies. In movies, we see characters with full human and artificial intelligence capabilities that can do anything. Real artificial intelligence, as it exists today, does not have the full capabilities of human intelligence. There are tasks that human intelligence performs best and other tasks that machines or artificial intelligence perform best. Just as our natural intelligence is made of multiple types of intelligence, so computers have their different types of intelligence. This is why numerous artificial intelligence technologies exist, each with its various capabilities.

Artificial intelligence outperforms our human intelligence for many tasks, but with some tasks that are basic for our human intelligence and abilities, artificial intelligence completely sucks. Therefore, real artificial intelligence cannot replace human intelligence today, but it can support human intelligence to achieve a more significant outcome.

ARTIFICIAL INTELLIGENCE FOR BUSINESS

In business, we use human intelligence and empower our capacities with computers and machines. Artificial intelligence will allow us to continue doing so, except that our computers, our machines, and tools get to be smarter now, therefore overtaking many tasks that humans used to do. This is partly what digital transformation is doing. Digital transformation is transforming the business landscape. Therefore, there is a need to reorganize—to rebalance the business or the organization's intelligence.

IS AI WORTH INVESTING IN NOW?

Every organization, every business should invest in AI, and the earlier, the better. AI is helping enterprises lead and repositioning them in powerful, efficient, and productive businesses. The pioneers are genuinely thriving, and their investments are paying more and more over time as they build cohesion, skills, data systems, and reinvent their business intelligence.

Investment in AI is a long-term investment in the basis and structure of today and tomorrow's business. AI investment does not involve AI technologies only. It includes investment in data, data science skills, business strategy, innovation strategy, and people transformation. The return on investment will increase significantly as the organization's intelligence increases in maturity, integration, and homogeneity.

HOW BUSINESSES ARE WINNING WITH AI

Many leading companies, small and large, from all types of industry have invested in artificial intelligence and are winning big with it.

Amazon is running its warehouses with robots day and night; it has a perfect combination of human and machine operational setting and is providing the best customer experience to stay number one.

Chatbots and automated telephone operators are standard in most businesses around the world. Now there are robots helping restaurants make pizza and prepare food while others are delivering room service in hotels. Alexa is answering many of our demands at home. Siri and other voice assistants have been assisting us for a while on our iPhones, smartphones, and computers. Identification and access control systems at home and in organizations are replacing our keys. Domotics or home automation is helping us having smarter homes and a more pleasant at-home experience. Smart city systems are helping in anticipating and managing public crises, while predictive and prescriptive health devices are helping physicians and health professionals to care for their patients. Artificial intelligence is a reality today, and many businesses are gaining leverage with it. You should leverage it for your business if you want to stay in business for the next five or ten years. Artificial intelligence is empowering every type of business—no exception.

Artificial intelligence, with its multiple technologies, has allowed businesses and organizations around the world to:

- Automate processes and deliver solutions faster and at a reduced cost
- Create new rewarding business models
- Anticipate business growth
- Predict outcomes
- Generate revenue streams that were not possible before
- Innovate and provide innovative products and services globally
- Create much-desired value that did not exist before

- Empower organizations to be more efficient and productive at once
- Improve customer experience
- Create more robust systems and organizations
- Empower individuals to develop their natural intelligence and grow
- Improve executive decision-making
- Decrease business risks

BUSINESSES SHOULD HAVE CLEAR GOALS FOR THEIR AI INVESTMENTS

For businesses to take advantage of AI, they must have an AI strategy and goals for implementing AI. I would even go further; they should have a digital transformation strategy that includes AI as a part of their transformation strategy. AI does not stand alone. Artificial intelligence will call for the full **digital transformation formula** as I promote in my books *The Digital Transformation Success Formula* and *Leveraging Digital Transformation.* I mean that it will require individuals in the organization, the business, and the technology to be transformed, all while keeping in check the fear factor for unleashing innovation.

AI IMPLEMENTATION REQUIRES TOP EXECUTIVES' INVOLVEMENT FOR SUCCESS

Experimenting with a small scale and isolated AI implementation project can be beneficial for a business, but it is not sustainable. In many cases, the small scale AI implementation may fail due to a lack of cohesion or alignment with other parts of the business. Therefore, it is essential to have an AI strategy that englobes the company.

AI, like other digital transformation enterprises, must be supported by top management because it will imply changes at multiple levels that require authority for critical decision-making. Therefore, AI is not to be implemented solely by the middle management because it would be an occasion for conflicts and misalignments between business units, which may lead to failure. Many businesses have encountered that kind of failure in their digital transformation journey over the years. Top executives' involvement is essential for this transformation to succeed.

THE HUMAN VS. MACHINE AI CHALLENGE FOR BUSINESS

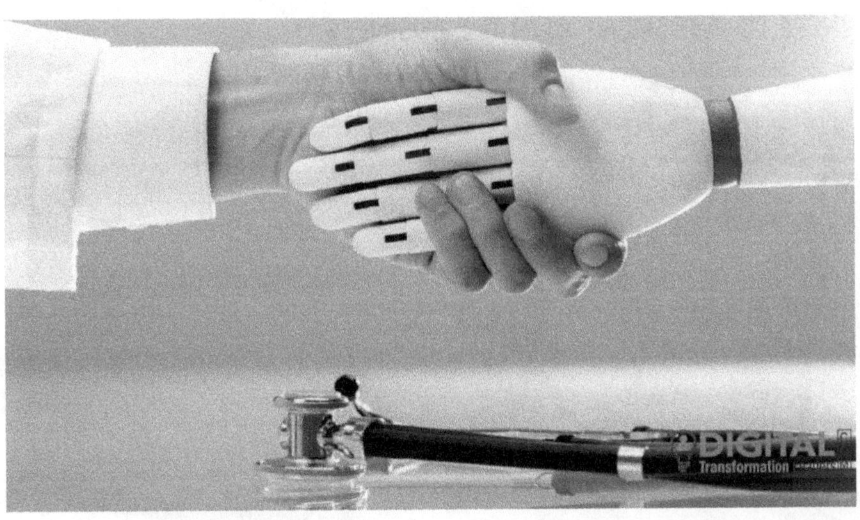

Implementing and using AI in any enterprise requires preparing the humans in the organization for a new way of collaborating and working with the machine. A mindset shift must happen, and we should address many unspoken fears. Unfortunately, many organizations overestimate the resistance power of humans and even their sabotaging capability when fearful. Implementing digital solutions without shifting the organization's mindset is a capital mistake made by most organizations that are experiencing failure or delay with transformation. It costs the organization in implementation speed, success, and the adoption of the new business intelligence.

The new business intelligence is not a machine, not a human. Today's successful digital intelligence is an efficient mix of human and machine intelligence. Humans must be both educated and prepared emotionally to collaborate with the machine, reducing fears to unleash innovation and creating outstanding value from the new business intelligence.

WHERE TO IMPLEMENT AI IN THE BUSINESS

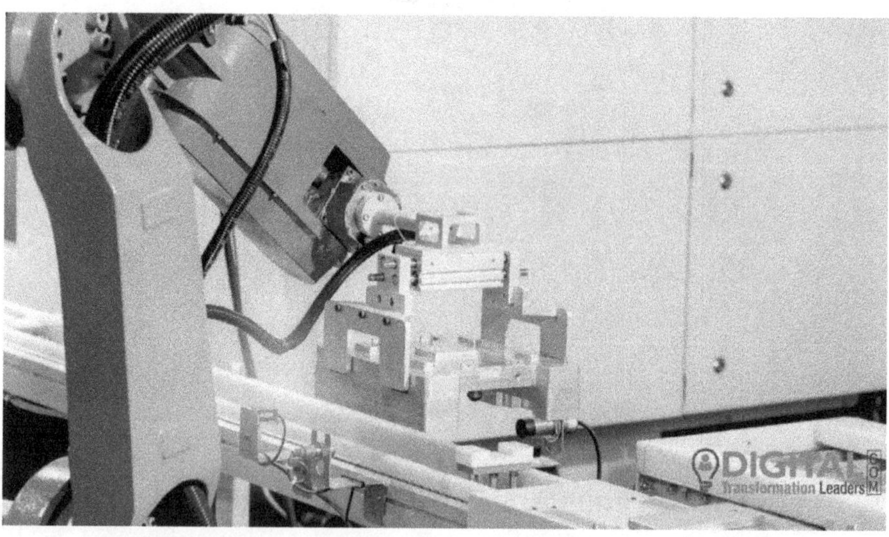

Real AI opportunities require looking at the business both from a helicopter view and with a microscopic view to identify opportunities for success with AI.

In transforming businesses, AI taps into the power of human intelligence but also into the power of data or data science. AI systems are made powerful with excellent data strategy. In some businesses, before investing in AI technologies, they must first invest in their processes and data approach to take advantage of AI.

One reason an AI implementation requires a tailor-made and insightful strategy is that artificial intelligence is not perfect as it is. Among the multiple types of intelligence that artificial intelligence includes, some areas are thriving and others are underperforming, but if their limitations are understood and correctly strategized for, businesses can win with them. Transforming with AI will benefit you not only from business strategy but also with your innovation skills.

It comes down to well-crafted recipes in terms of strategies and the choice of the right technologies for the business and the business context. It pays to team up with expert advisors, and I would be happy to support you and your business.

AI AND JOB LOSS—DON'T FIRE EVERYONE YET

If AI suppresses the need for many tasks and, therefore, jobs, AI also brings excellent job opportunities for hiring new specialists as well as reinventing people's careers. It is an opportunity for employees who may have been made redundant in the organization, and it may be time that they review their career goals. So, don't just fire all redundant employees yet. You'll most likely need their business expertise, and you can train them (or many of them) for serving the enterprise at another level, at the condition that they can handle change. This is especially true if you will be implementing any machine learning AI implementation.

CHANGE MANAGEMENT IS A MUST-HAVE SKILL FOR EVERY ORGANIZATION

Changes in the professions, digital transformation, and in particular, the use of artificial intelligence are the reasons why every organization should first invest in their employees. Every organization wins in some way by helping its people embrace change, learn, and develop new skills; their employees will then help them thrive and innovate in the digital economy.

Many organizations complain that their people are inflexible, but they have not invested in them or supported them in adopting change. This is a crucial thing because the digital age is about change and transformation, and any business with people who cannot embrace change, cannot innovate and, therefore, will likely disappear. Managing change is the essential skill every organization should offer to its people at every level.

People with the business expertise who are trained to embrace change are among a business' greatest assets. With additional professional skills, they will drive AI innovation and transformation in the organization.

Let's take machine learning, for example; it is a discipline of AI that requires the business or professional knowledge to help the machine deliver a more excellent outcome. In organizations where the people with expert knowledge are laid off, it is more challenging to implement an effective machine learning project. The same goes for the data strategy; we need professional and business expertise to implement the best data strategy to amplify artificial intelligence benefits and achievements.

So don't just fire most of the workforce and depend entirely on machines, no matter what an AI salesperson told you. For most AI systems, you need both human professional skills and intelligence, along with artificial intelligence for the greatest success, and people who know your business and the organization already can be a great asset if you invest in their individual and professional transformation. Now, you may not need all the people you had before rebalancing the organization's intelligence, but you'll need some for each unit.

AI IMPLEMENTATION SHOULD CONSIDER THE CONTEXT AND SURROUNDINGS

While the self-driving car is ready and available, putting it in an unknown environment with many unpredictable and chaotic possibilities, such as today's cities' heavy traffic with pedestrians and different types of mobility machines, will cause it to fail. The failure will be because the environment is not adapted or mapped for self-driving cars.

Putting the self-driving car in an environment prepared for it, such as airports, campuses, and other controlled private sites, will cause it to work perfectly. The same goes for introducing robots and any other AI technologies in business. The business context and the environment should be considered for a safe and harmonious collaboration.

FACILITATE AI PROJECT SUCCESS

With different AI technologies for business processes, business units, and cross-operation, businesses and organizations will implement AI through multiple projects for the AI enterprise implementation. It is imperative to keep these projects aligned for the whole organization, no matter how the business chooses to structure the implementations. Without the master roadmap for all AI initiatives, the organization may soon become confused about what it is trying to achieve.

AI integrations between systems must be well thought out and planned across several business units, organizations, or teams. The business strategy and executive involvement are of utmost importance. A manager may not be able to see the impact of changes on every other unit. However, every business unit must be aligned, and in the adverse situation, a leader in top management can decide which direction to go based on all information made available.

CHOOSING AI TECHNOLOGIES

More and more AI technologies are made available on the market today. Some are very straightforward and ready to configure and use right away, while others are to be programmed and genuinely customized for the business. Machine learning solutions, for example, are and will be more available for enterprises, and these enterprises will have to teach the machine what to do. It can go from simple to more complex algorithms.

It is essential that every organization consider its objectives and goals and qualifies the technology before making a choice. If no specialist is available in-house, the organization should enlist the help of professional AI consultants who can help them select the right products to align with their AI strategies and goals.

DO YOU KNOW YOUR BUSINESS PROCESSES?

Before choosing business technologies, the processes must be analyzed and considered for optimization before choosing AI technologies. For some operations, several AI technologies will need to work together to deliver the outcome. Further analysis should be carried out to evaluate the existing processes and maybe upgrade them or create new ones. There is an alignment to do, and it must go into business details to avoid bad surprises later.

As a senior consultant with experiences in several sectors, I have seen many hidden sub-processes or exceptions to handle in every business. Sometimes even the business experts are not conscious of that, or they forget to mention them in their documentation or routine procedures explanations. It takes a great strategic consultant to ask the right questions, go into detail, challenge processes, and team up with the process owner or professional person to address some features that may have significant business impacts.

AI allows us to automate many processes, but any flaw we give it may amplify it.

ETHICAL AND LEGAL ISSUES WITH AI

As with every powerful technology, both ethical and legal concerns need to be addressed in adopting AI for business. There are points that relate to our conscious choices and others that relate to legal aspects. Laws and tolerability are different in different countries and regions. The AI strategies must address the legal aspects of the countries of business (now internationally or globally) and particularly when it comes to individual and business privacy. For cross-countries implementation, strategies must be taken into account along with the boundaries and authorization of the different territories involved. As AI develops further, the legal aspects of diverse practices must be monitored as well to remain within the legalities and avoid any negative repercussions for the business.

Many AI aspects are not yet legalized in many countries. However, this situation is changing as we achieve more innovation with AI. So it would be best to have someone who keeps their eyes open on AI legalities in one or more jurisdictions.

THE NEW BUSINESS INTELLIGENCE

Every business should implement AI in their organization, and they should not focus on AI only, but on creating new business intelligence, which is a combination of human intelligence and artificial intelligence. They should balance it so that the different types of intelligence support each other in delivering more powerful business outcomes and competitive innovation. So implementing AI just as a technology implementation is not the right approach for successful AI implementation and adoption. Think in terms of new business intelligence.

HOW TO GET STARTED IN AI NOW AND BE SUPPORTED

To start or improve your AI strategy and implementation, get help creating your AI roadmap, or even get a second opinion. I would be pleased to assist you in different ways.

1. You may hire me as an advisor. I am an **MIT Sloan & MIT CSAIL Certified AI Strategist**, and also **MIT Sloan School of Management** certified in **Executive Strategy and Innovation**. You can count on my senior IT and Business Management consultant experience of **twenty-plus years, internationally transforming organizations**. You may book a complimentary executive alignment meeting with me in my calendar: https://calendly.com/mnadiavincent/ai-executive-alignment
2. You may join my exclusive executive only Executive Innovators Board membership platform to find practical professional resources and "know-how" that you can implement in your organization. Executive Innovators Board is also a mastermind

group with a monthly meeting to answer the challenges you are facing in your transformation journey. More info here: https://www.digitaltransformationleaders.com/pages/the-executive-innovators-boardroom

I wish you and your organization much success in your journey to implement AI.

BIBLIOGRAPHY

Anders, George. "Inside Amazon's Idea Machine: How Bezos Decodes Customers." *Forbes*. April 23, 2012. http://www.forbes.com/sites/georgeanders/2012/04/04/inside-amazon/#371ad55e7ae2

Big Data Made Simple: Big Data Definition. http://bigdata-madesimple.com/. Accessed July 2016.

Christensen, Clayton M. and Hal B. Gregersen. *The Innovator's DNA: Mastering the Five Skills of Disruptive Innovators.*

Davenport, Thomas H and D. J. Patil. "Data Scientist: The Sexiest Job of the 21st Century." *Harvard Business Review.* (Oct 2012) https://hbr.org/2012/10/data-scientist-the-sexiest-job-of-the-21st-century

Gartner IT Glossary, Big Data. http://www.gartner.com/it-glossary/big-data/. Accessed October 2016.

ABOUT THE AUTHOR

M. NADIA VINCENT is an author, professional keynote speaker, leadership coach, and digital transformation leadership consultant. She earned a Master of Business Administration (MBA) degree from UBI with a specialization in IT Management. Nadia also is a Massachusetts Institute of Technology (MIT) Certified Digital Transformation Executive Advisor. She holds two MIT Sloan School of Management Executive Certificates respectively in Strategy and Innovation and in Management and Leadership. Furthermore, Nadia is also MIT certified in Artificial Intelligence Executive Advising.

Nadia is the author of the book *Leveraging Digital Transformation; Proven Leadership and Innovation Strategies to Engage and Grow Your Organization*. Strategic, results-oriented, empathetic, and creative, she is on a mission to help executives and organizations transform their businesses, improve team performance, innovate, and succeed in the digital age while improving individual happiness.

Nadia travels throughout the world delivering speaking engagements related to leadership, change management, digital transformation, and innovation. She fluently speaks English, French, Spanish, and Creole. An accomplished project/program manager, speaker, and trainer, over the years, Nadia has developed many training and coaching programs for various international organizations. She is also a regular PMI Global contributor and trainer.

A global IT Management Consultant with over two decades of experience in the American and European continents with Fortune 500 companies, Nadia possesses great experience managing high profile business transformation projects, including leading international and offshore teams, in different sectors. She has led and implemented many business and IT transformation projects in industries such as international banking, trading and settlement, financial services, energy distribution, electronic payments, insurance, European airline traffic control, retail market, petrol distribution, and the European government.

Originally from the Caribbean, Nadia has lived and worked in numerous countries throughout the world, and currently resides in Brussels, Belgium.

ABOUT M. NADIA VINCENT TRAINING AND COACHING

Nadia helps organization implement digital transformation by providing hands on learning and coaching experiences for managers and leaders who are responsible of implementing organizational change.

She has three main learning categories for managers:

1. Self-transformation: promoting individual transformation for organizational transformation.
2. Digital Transformation leadership: The main course for implementing digital transformation.
3. Executive Innovators Board: Executive Innovators Board is the ultimate digital transformation executive coaching library and world-class mastermind group, with outstanding value for high achieving executives. In EIB, all aspects of digital transformation leadership and all aspects of business transformation are covered. The content is evolutive and participants access EIB through a yearly membership.

Each category contains several courses that can be followed on demand.

The main course for implementing digital transformation offers a transformation leaders' mastermind group that meets monthly to address challenges that managers encounter as they implement transformation in their organizations and find solutions.

Executive Innovators Board is the main program with the most value. It focuses on developing effective digital executives, and covers management and leadership, business and innovation strategy, organizational transformation, technology transformation, self-transformation, and well-being.

Please find out more on www.DigitalTransformationLeaders.com.

ABOUT EXECUTIVE INNOVATORS BOARD

Nadia Vincent offers an exclusive, membership-only access for executive clients who want to be inspired, supported, and continue to learn as they transform their organizations.

Executives are the captains of their organizations and the creators of destinies. Executive Innovators Board supports executives as they navigate the challenging waters of digital transformation.

Executive Advantage includes resources and support for:

- Innovating in your organization

Learn digital innovation strategies, and turn your organization into a winning digital innovator on multiple levels, regardless of your industry.

- Leading and managing transformation

Management and leadership principles, best practices, and proven know-how to guide you as you lead your organization to digital success.

- Transforming for success

Proven solutions for the multiple aspects of the transformation process, business and technology transformation, self-transformation, and inspiring your organization to transform while supporting individual transformation.

If this is something you are interested in, you can review some of the resources of the Executive Innovators Board below at this time:

1. Creating and implementing your digital strategy for the brightest future
2. Solving digital transformation challenges
3. Optimizing and automating business processes
4. Neuroplasticity for executives
5. Transforming your organization for business success
6. Negotiating partnership deals for business transformation
7. Developing your technology transformation strategy
8. Transforming with AI
9. Innovating for breakthrough
10. Creating a successful transformation roadmap
11. Executive leadership for transformation
12. Creating a successful customer experience
13. Rewarding business models and revenue strategies to grow your business
14. Implementing enterprise-wide digital transformation

Executive Innovators Board launches onJanuary 6th, 2020.

Besides all the resources, Executive Innovators Board has a monthly webinar where we address different realities and challenges of digital transformation and how to solve them.

The Executive Innovators:

Executive Innovators Board answers the continuous demand for Digital Executives. Nadia herself is a continuous learner and alumni at MIT Sloan Executive Education, where she follows some of the best programs and advising from MIT Sloan Executive Education related to digital transformation, notably in management, innovation strategy, and technology.

To join, simply go to www.DigitalTransformationLeaders.com and select Executive Innovators Board.

ABOUT M. NADIA VINCENT EXECUTIVE ADVISORY & CONSULTING SERVICES

Our clients can count on us for the following services as well as "2nd advice" for any of the listed services.

1. Strategic Artificial Intelligence Transformation Advising
   - AI Business Strategy & Roadmap
   - AI Strategy Implementation
   - AI Tools Selection
   - AI 2nd Advice

2. Innovative Digital Transformation Advising & Consulting
   - Business Transformation (BT) Strategy & Roadmap
   - BT Strategy Implementation

– Technology Strategy
– Data Strategy
– Strategic Innovation
– Customer Experience and Loyalty
– Business Models
– Revenue Models
– Innovation for Mature Products and Services
– Disruptive Innovation
– Organizational Transformation

Nadia Vincent offers a complimentary thirty-minute alignment meeting online for every executive who is interested in her executive advisory services. You may book the meeting directly in her calendar from the website:

https://www.DigitalTransformationLeaders.com/pages/executive-advisory-support-services

BOOK M. NADIA VINCENT TO SPEAK AT YOUR NEXT EVENT

When it comes to choosing a professional keynote speaker for your next event, you will find no one more experienced, tried, and tested—no one who will leave your audience or colleagues with a more renewed passion for digital transformation, leadership, and the necessity to own one's destiny in the digital age—than Nadia Vincent.

Nadia has delivered many inspirational presentations worldwide for multiple organizations. Whether your audience is ten or 10,000, in North America, South America, Europe, or elsewhere, Nadia Vincent can deliver a customized message of inspiration to your organization or conference.

Nadia understands that your audience does not want to be "taught" anything, but rather is interested in hearing real digital transformation stories of inspiration, achievement, and real-life people stepping into their destinies. As a result, Nadia Vincent's speaking philosophy is to entertain and inspire your audience with passion, humor, and stories proven to help people achieve extraordinary results.

If you are looking for a memorable speaker who will leave your audience wanting more, book Nadia Vincent today! To see a highlight video of Nadia Vincent and see if she is available for your next meeting or event, visit her website at the address below. Then contact her by phone or email to schedule a complimentary, pre-speech phone interview.

www.DigitalTransformationLeaders.com

www.ingramcontent.com/pod-product-compliance
Lightning Source LLC
LaVergne TN
LVHW092007050326
832904LV00021B/335/J
* 9 7 8 1 9 5 0 2 4 1 5 2 1 *